ACCLAIM FOR
God and Sex

"GOD AND SEX offers the best scholarship on a topic of timeless fascination in a form that's engaging for general readers, but also brings information that may surprise even some scholars." —*Publishers Weekly*

"Here a seasoned interpreter of Scripture shows how ancient authors viewed the world of sexuality, and how these ancient reflections can influence modern thinking [on] issues ranging from adultery and premarital sex to same-sex relations and heterosexual sex within marriage." —Bart D. Ehrman, *New York Times* bestselling author of *Misquoting Jesus*

"Michael Coogan's excellent book is a reminder that the Bible cuts both ways, and that in the right hands it might once again become a force for positive social change." —*Toronto Globe and Mail*

"Michael Coogan is an extraordinary writer on the culture of the Bible and the ancient Near East...He always manages to make his scholarship accessible to the general reader. It's hard to imagine readers not being interested in the subject of sex and God, especially in the hands of a writer as skillful as Coogan."
—Thomas Cahill, former director of religious publishing at Doubleday and author of the bestselling Hinges of History series

"A critique as radical as this one will astonish conservatives...It will embolden social activists glad to weaken restraints rooted in traditional understandings of scripture. Expect media attention and controversy."
—*Booklist*

"Quick, clear, and no-nonsense...Coogan's chapters [are] arranged with more care than much of Scripture."
—PopMatters.com

God and Sex

What the Bible Really Says

Michael Coogan

TWELVE

NEW YORK BOSTON

Twelve
Hachette Book Group
1290 Avenue of the Americas
New York, NY 10104

www.HachetteBookGroup.com

Twelve is an imprint of Grand Central Publishing.
The Twelve name and logo are trademarks of Hachette Book Group, Inc.

The publisher is not responsible for websites (or their content) that are not owned by the publisher.

Originally published in hardcover by Twelve.

First Trade Edition: November 2011

The Library of Congress has cataloged the hardcover edition as follows:

Coogan, Michael David.
    God and sex : what the Bible really says / Michael Coogan. – 1st ed.
        p. cm.
    Includes index.
    ISBN 978-0-446-54525-9
    1. Sex in the Bible.   I. Title.
    BS680.S5C645 2010
    220.8'3067–dc22

                                                            2010004795

ISBN 978-0-446-54526-6 (pbk.)

For Pam
with love
as always

CONTENTS

Introduction   xi

1. **To Know in the Biblical Sense: Speaking of Sex**   1

2. **He Will Rule over You: The Status of Women**   19
   Widows   26
   Virginity   27
      Jephthah's Virgin Daughter   28
      Celibacy as an Ideal   32
      The Virgin Mary   36
   Women's Public Roles   39
   Women's Domestic Roles   50

3. **As It Was in the Beginning?: Marriage and Divorce**   61
   Abortion   64
   Arranged Marriages   67
   Endogamy and Exogamy   70
   Polygamy   73
   Divorce   84

CONTENTS

4. **Thou Shalt Not: Forbidden Sexual Relationships in the Bible**   99

   Adultery   101
   David and Bathsheba   104
   Sex with Family Members   108
   Tamar   110
   Lot's Daughters   113
   Reuben   114
   Other Prohibited Sexual Relationships   115
   Same-Sex Relationships in the Bible   117
   David and Jonathan   118
   Sodom and Sodomy   121
   Prohibitions of Homoerotic Relations   134
   Jesus and Same-Sex Relationships   139

5. **Folly in Israel: Rape and Prostitution**   141
   Dinah   147
   Tamar   149
   Prostitution   150

6. **Fire in the Divine Loins: God's Wives in Myth and Metaphor**   161
   Myth and Metaphor   165
   Yahweh's Wives in Myth   166
   Polytheism in Ancient Israel   170
   Yahweh's Children   176
   The Goddess Wisdom   178
   Yahweh's Wives in Metaphor   181
   Problems with the Metaphor   186

CONTENTS

Conclusion   189

Acknowledgments   196

Illustration Credits   197

Bibliography   198

Notes   202

Index   229

INTRODUCTION

The Bible is constantly in the news. Pastors and popes, politicians and pundits regularly cite it as an unchallenge- able authority on all sorts of issues, to undergird widely divergent points of view. In the United States especially, where more than ninety percent of homes have a Bible,[1] that very old book is regularly cited in the culture wars about "family values," most of which have to do with issues of sex and gender.

At its biennial assembly in August 2009, the Evangelical Lutheran Church in America debated and ultimately approved a resolution allowing its clergy to have "lifelong, monogamous, same-gender relationships."[2] In doing so it joined other liberal Jewish and Christian groups in giving religious sanction to same-sex marriages, now legal in five states and seven countries, and, more broadly, to same-sex civil unions or domestic partnerships, recognized in dozens of jurisdictions worldwide. Reaction from conservative Lutherans and others was swift and unequivocal: the decision was heretical, even pagan, because it was contrary to God's word as revealed in the Bible. Yet proponents of the decision, as of similar actions by other religious groups, also claimed that their views were consistent with biblical teaching. News reports about the Lutherans' meeting spoke of "dueling Bible verses."[3]

As a resident of Massachusetts, I have had a front-row seat for the controversy concerning same-sex marriage. In 2003, that state's highest court ruled that prohibiting same-sex couples from marrying violated the Massachusetts Constitution.[4] In the subsequent and ongoing national debate, as a biblical scholar I was both amused and troubled by the use of the Bible in arguments against such marriage. As one catchy slogan put it, in the Garden of Eden there were Adam and Eve, not Adam and Steve. And, from the beginning,[5] it was claimed, marriage has been between one man and one woman; in fact, not until late in the biblical period was monogamy the norm. But despite their exaggerations, opponents of same-sex marriage, and of homosexuality in general, much like the advocates of slavery in the nineteenth century, have biblical authority on their side, to a point. Yet the other sides in these debates also have appealed to the Bible in support of their views, and they too are right, also to a point.

But what is the Bible? Although the very word "bible" means "book," the Bible was not delivered to humanity as a complete book, written by God and shrink-wrapped in a shipment from Amazon or available for download on a Kindle or an iPad. Rather, the Bible is an anthology, a selection of texts from ancient Israel, early Judaism, and, for Christians, from the first hundred years or so of Christianity. Those texts are called books, and like other books, they have human authors, many of whom are identified as such in the books themselves: Amos, Isaiah, Jeremiah, and Paul, for example. Sometimes the books also describe the process of how they were written down. So, the prophet Jeremiah twice dictates his words to his scribe Baruch,[6] and Paul, having dictated the body of one of several letters he wrote to Christians in the Greek city of Corinth, added a postscript in his own handwriting.[7] These books were written over the course of many centuries, and, like all other books, they reflect the presuppositions and prejudices, the ideas and ideals of their authors (almost entirely men) and of the societies in and for which they were written.

Similar to other anthologies, the Bible is selective—it is not a complete collection. Biblical writers often refer to other books that they used as sources. My personal favorite is the Book of the Wars of the LORD, mentioned as the source of an ancient poem quoted in the book of Numbers.[8] The Book of the Wars of the LORD is not preserved in the Bible, nor has it yet been found by archaeologists or treasure hunters, but how I would love to be able to read it. Similarly, Paul refers to several letters he wrote to the Corinthians, but only two of them are preserved in the New Testament.[9] So, it turns out, the Bible has sources, only some of which were incorporated into its books. Likewise, only some of the sacred writings of ancient Israel, early Judaism, and early Christianity were included in what became the Bible, the canonical scriptures deemed to have a special authority. We can make educated guesses about why some writings were omitted. Some were probably considered heretical by religious leaders as they formed their canons, and others may not have had a proper pedigree. Many of these noncanonical writings have survived, however, and they shed important light on the background of the books of the Bible.

The authors of those books were in essence interpreting their experience of God and its implications for their lives. For the ancient Israelites, that God was Yahweh, conventionally rendered "the LORD" and worshipped continually ever since by Jews, Christians, and Muslims under different names and titles. As Yahweh, he is reported to have revealed himself to Abraham, Moses, the prophets, and others. But these putative revelations are often inconsistent. For example, in the Ten Commandments, Yahweh declares that he punishes sons for the sins of their fathers to the third and fourth generation.[10] But centuries later, speaking to the prophet Ezekiel, he seems to have changed his mind:

> A son shall not suffer for a father's iniquity, nor shall
> a father suffer for a son's iniquity; the righteousness
> of the righteous shall be his own, and the wicked-
> ness of the wicked shall be his own.[11]

Clearly, different writers had different views. Inconsistencies like these require first that readers of the Bible who consider it authoritative read all of it, not blithely picking only passages that coincide with their own views. Second, such inconsistencies invite, even demand inter- pretation: if scripture itself reflects developing or at least differing views, then its readers must scrutinize them carefully, critically. This is especially true given the profound influence the Bible enjoys.

Unraveling the complicated history of the formation of the Bible has been the substance of the work of biblical scholars since the Enlightenment. They—or rather, we—have been able to trace the development of biblical religion and its various schools of thought, and have posited multiple sources within the Bible itself to explain its repetitions and inconsistencies. A majority of biblical scholars agree on both methods and results. But unhap- pily we have not succeeded in changing the way most nonspecialists and even many in the clergy think about the Bible. People still maintain that the Bible is God's word, plain and simple: that God is the author of scrip- ture. Even nonscholars can see problems with this. If God wrote the Bible, he is a forgetful writer. Did he give Moses the Ten Commandments on Mount Sinai or Mount Horeb? Did David kill Goliath or did Elhanan? Was the Last Supper a Passover meal or not? For each of these ques- tions and innumerable others, the Bible gives more than one answer. If God wrote the Bible, he is also a terrible writer—over and over, the same story is told and retold, with many changes and in wildly divergent styles. These inconsistencies and repetitions can only be explained by multiple human authors. It is their writings that were collected into the mini-library that eventually became the Bible, and their writings that need to be interpreted.

I have written this book because of a conviction that biblical scholars have a responsibility to explore the significance of their findings for a larger audience. Scholars' timidity, I think, frequently inhibits them from presenting what they think about the relevance of the Bible for contemporary issues. Too often the field is left to amateurs, the hyperpious, and crazies—and when the Bible is the subject, there are plenty of every type. My specific focus is on sex in the Bible, both human and divine, and on the related category of gender. What did the many biblical writers think about sexual morality and about the roles of men and women? How were their views informed by their own cultural presuppositions? Are they consistent? Are they still relevant?

So, this is a book about how to read and use the Bible, with a focus on "family values." A wise colleague once observed that there is sex on every page of the Bible if you just know where to look. In the chapters that follow, we will find sex in places where people do not usually see it. We will explore the mysteries of "love as strong as death."[12] We will examine the views of biblical writers, often different from our own, and often problematic. We will look at how biblical teachings have been appropriated, adapted, and sometimes rejected through history. And we will consider how the Bible may have enduring significance.

CHAPTER 1

TO KNOW IN THE BIBLICAL SENSE

Speaking of Sex

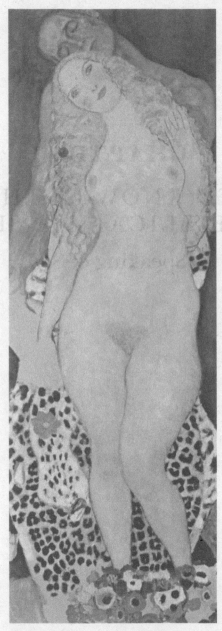

Gustav Klimt, *Adam and Eve,*
1917–1918 (unfinished).

"The past is a foreign country: they do things differently there." Those are the opening words of L. P. Hartley's novel *The Go-Between*,[1] in which a middle-aged man discovers a diary he had written when he was twelve. The past in his case is his own past. But it is an epigram that historians often quote, with good reason: in studying the past, we have to learn how they did things there, being careful not to project our own values and social constructs onto other cultures, and recognizing that words can have different meanings and nuances.

In looking at the Bible, we need to realize that we are entering a foreign country. Its languages, cultures, and values, although in some ways apparently familiar because of the status of the Bible in Judaism and Christianity, differ in many ways from our own. Even the treatment of a universal human experience such as sex is culturally specific in the biblical world. Here is an example, from the Song of Solomon, a series of exotic and erotic love poems. In it, two lovers describe each other's bodies. First, the man describes his beloved, moving downward from the head.

> How beautiful you are, my love,
>   how very beautiful!
> Your eyes are doves
>   behind your veil.
> Your hair is like a flock of goats,
>   streaming down from Mount Gilead.
> Your teeth are like a flock of shorn ewes
>   that have come up from the washing;
> all of them have twins:
>   and none of them has lost a lamb.
> Your lips are like a crimson thread,
>   and your mouth is lovely.
> Your temples are like halves of a pomegranate
>   behind your veil.
> Your neck is like David's tower,
>   built in courses;
> on it hang a thousand shields,
>   all of them warriors' armor.
> Your two breasts are like two fawns,
>   twins of a gazelle,
>   grazing among the lilies.
> Until the day breathes
>   and the shadows flee,
> I will make my way to the mount of myrrh
>   and to the hill of frankincense.

All of you is beautiful, my love;
    there is no flaw in you.[2]

Later, he continues, moving upward from the feet.

How beautiful are your feet in sandals,
    O daughter of a prince!
Your curved hips are like jewelry,
    the work of an artisan's hands.
Your hollow[3] is a rounded bowl
    that does not lack mixed wine.
Your belly is a heap of wheat,
    encircled by lilies.
Your two breasts are like two fawns,
    twins of a gazelle.
Your neck is like an ivory tower.
Your eyes are pools in Heshbon,
    by the gate of Bath-rabbim.
Your nose is like a tower of Lebanon,
    overlooking Damascus.
Your head—upon you like Carmel,
    and the locks of your head like purple;
    a king is held captive in the tresses.[4]

But this is not just male voyeurism; the woman also describes her lover, although with somewhat less anatomical detail.

My beloved is radiant and ruddy,
    prominent among ten thousand.
His head is gold, pure gold;
    his locks are palm shoots

black as a raven.
His eyes are like doves
    beside streams of water,
bathing in milk,
    sitting by a pool.
His cheeks are like beds of balsam,
    wafting fragrant aromas.
His lips are lilies,
    dripping with liquid myrrh.
His arms are rods of gold,
    studded with gems from Tarshish.
His loins are ivory plaques,
    overlaid with lapis lazuli.
His thighs are alabaster columns,
    set upon bases of gold.
His appearance is like Lebanon,
    choice as the cedars.
His mouth is most sweet:
    all of him is desirable.
This is my beloved and this is my love,
    O daughters of Jerusalem.[5]

These descriptions of bodies are universal expressions of sexual attraction: every detail of the beloved's body captivates the lover. Yet they also give us a window into a world very different from ours, one with exotic flora and fauna, a dramatic topography, and distinct views of beauty as well: would any man today dare to compare his beloved's nose to a mountain tower or her hair to a flock of goats?

In the biblical past, as in foreign countries, not only did they do things differently, they also spoke different languages, languages with distinct idioms, including those used for sex. One familiar biblical idiom for having sexual intercourse is "knowing"—"to know in the biblical sense," as the phrase has it, means to have sex with. The Hebrew verb translated as "know" can, and usually does, refer to what we would call intellectual knowledge, but more than a dozen times in the Bible it has the sense of the intimate knowledge that occurs during sexual intercourse—"carnal knowledge." So, after their expulsion from the Garden of Eden, the man (soon to be called Adam) "knew his wife Eve, and she became pregnant, and gave birth to Cain."[6] Similarly, in the rules for warfare, the Israelites reportedly killed enemy populations: all the men, of every age, and all the women except virgins, "those who had not known a man by sleeping with a male."[7]

Some modern translations of the Bible render the verb that literally means "know" dynamically in these contexts—"lie with," or "have relations with," or "have sexual intercourse with." These are accurate paraphrases, but they prevent readers from recognizing sexual nuance when the verb "know" is used elsewhere. For example, speaking in the name of the LORD, the prophet Amos tells the Israelites, "You only have I known of all the families of the earth."[8] For Amos, God and Israel had a unique relationship that metaphorically had an intimate dimension: Israel was God's bride and he was her lover, her husband, who "knew" her.

The sexual connotation of "knowing" sheds light on one level of meaning in the story of the Garden of Eden, where the man and the woman eat from the "tree of knowledge of good and evil." What was the forbidden fruit in Eden? We get a clue in an episode in King David's life. During his son Absalom's revolt against him, David was forced to flee his capital, Jerusalem, and stayed in exile in Transjordan with a loyal and wealthy subject named Barzillai. After Absalom had been defeated, David returned to Jerusalem to reclaim his throne. He was accompanied by Barzillai as far as the Jordan River, where David said to Barzillai:

> "Cross over with me, and I will provide for you with me in Jerusalem." But Barzillai said to the king, "How many are the days of the years of my life that I should go up with the king to Jerusalem? Today is my eightieth birthday; can I know between good and evil? Can your servant taste what he eats and what he drinks? Can I still hear the sounds of singing men and singing women? Why then should your servant be an added burden to my lord the king?"[9]

As a reward for Barzillai's faithful service, the king was offering him the pleasures of the court: royal feasts, royal musicians, and "good and evil," which I interpret as the royal harem—in other words, wine, women, and song. But Barzillai, at an advanced age for that time, claimed to be too old to enjoy any of these pleasures.

So, in the Garden of Eden the man and the woman ate from the tree of knowledge of good and evil. There is another circumlocution here, for eating is a widespread euphemism for sex, as a biblical proverb shows.

> This is the way of a woman committing adultery:
> she eats, and wipes her mouth,
> and says: "I have done nothing wrong."[10]

Obviously the proverb concerns far more than table etiquette. When the man and the woman ate the forbidden fruit, they immediately recognized that they were naked. There was no sex education in the Garden—it was only "Adam and maiden," in Dylan Thomas's phrasing. Their first sexual experience was a revelation: they now "knew" what they had not known before, including their sexual nature, so they covered themselves with what would become the proverbial fig leaves. To be sure, to understand eating the fruit of the tree of knowledge of good and evil as sexual intercourse is only one possible interpretation. It does not exclude others: in the Bible as in literature generally, multiple levels of meaning, including sexual innuendo, are frequently present, often deliberately so.

Other references to sexual intercourse also use ordinary words with a specifically sexual sense. Among the most frequent is a Hebrew verb that means "to lie with" or "to sleep with," with both primary and sexual meanings parallel to English usage. Another verb means "to go to, to go into, to enter," understood literally. Both verbs can be used independently, and sometimes they are used together, making the meaning transparent. For example, Rachel, Jacob's favorite wife, was childless, while her older sister Leah, the first of his several wives, had already produced four sons for him. One of them, Reuben, had found some mandrakes in the field, a plant thought in many cultures to be an aphrodisiac and to enhance fertility: "Get with child a mandrake root" is how John Donne incredulously put it. Desperate to have a child, Rachel promised Leah a night with their husband in exchange for the mandrakes. She said to her sister, "He may lie with you tonight," and Leah then informed Jacob, "You must come into me."[11] Similarly, the spies whom Joshua had sent to reconnoiter the land around Jericho went to the house of a prostitute named Rahab and "lay" there, and when the king of Jericho learned of it, he told her to "bring out the men who went into you."[12]

Another term for sexual intercourse is "uncovering the nakedness," used repeatedly in a long list of persons with whom intercourse is prohibited: the mother, the sister, the aunt, daughter-in-law, sister-in-law, and so on.[13] "Nakedness" means both male and female genitals, as do several parts of the lower extremities of the body in their vicinity, such as loins, thigh, heel, and especially feet, another frequent euphemism. For example, in the Bible as in other ancient literature we find vivid descriptions of the horrors of ancient siege warfare. One such description, anticipating the destruction of Jerusalem as divine punishment for the Israelites' disobedience, warns that in those dire days a woman will eat her placenta, "the afterbirth that comes out from between her feet."[14] Using the same euphemism, the prophet Isaiah proclaims that Yahweh will punish the Israelites through the king of Assyria, who will shave off all their body hair—"the head, the hair of the feet, and even the beard"[15]—symbolically reducing them to weak prepubescent boys.

We also find "feet" with the meaning "genitals" in the book of Ruth, whose heroine, a widow, wants to marry a wealthy relative, Boaz. As he was sleeping in his field during the fall harvest, at midnight she "uncovered his feet." Startled—and not because his toes were cold—he said, "Who are you?" She answered, "I am Ruth, your servant. Spread your cloak over your servant, for you are my legal next of kin." He invited her to spend the night, and she "lay at his feet" until before dawn.[16]

Likewise, one of the heroines of Israel's history in the late second millennium BCE, as recounted in the book of Judges, is Jael, wife of Heber the Kenite. According to the prose version of her story in chapter 4, after a battle in which the Israelites had defeated the Canaanites, she invited the fleeing Canaanite commander, Sisera, into her tent and gave him milk to quench his thirst. When he fell asleep, exhausted, she killed him, driving a tent peg through his temple.[17] But there is an older, poetic version of this episode in the next chapter, the famous Song of Deborah, and according to it:

> Between her feet he knelt down,
> > he fell, he lay:
> where he knelt down, there he fell, wasted.[18]

The ancient poem implies that Jael seduced Sisera and then killed him as he slept in postcoital fatigue, a sexual innuendo that the later prose writer omitted.

The word "feet" has a similar meaning in a brief story about Moses and his wife Zipporah. Early in his adult life, Moses had fled Egyptian jurisdiction because he had committed a murder. But when God appeared to Moses in the burning bush in the desert, he commanded him to return to Egypt and lead the Israelites from there to the Promised Land. A reluctant prophet, Moses made a series of objections to the divine call, but in the end God persuaded him to agree. As he was en route back to Egypt, at a place where he, Zipporah, and their young son were spending the night, "Yahweh met him and tried to kill him." This mysterious—not to say irrational—deity is here depicted as a malevolent night demon, as elsewhere in the Bible—earlier, he had similarly attacked Jacob at night,[19] and he will do the same to the Egyptians on the terrible night of the tenth plague, the killing of all the firstborn in the land of Egypt, "from the firstborn of

Pharaoh sitting on his throne to the firstborn of the slave woman grinding at the mill and the firstborn of all the animals."[20] To ward off this night-stalking deity, the Israelites would smear their door frames with lamb's blood, just as they would later attach to their doors an amulet—the mezuzah—to keep him at bay.

So Yahweh tried to kill Moses, but why? Zipporah apparently knew the reason—because Moses was uncircumcised. And she knew what to do:

> She took a flint and cut off her son's foreskin, and touched his [Moses's] feet with it, and said, "Truly you are a bridegroom of blood to me!" So he let him alone. It was then she said, "A bridegroom of blood by circumcision."[21]

Zipporah, to paraphrase, took the bloody piece of skin that she had deftly removed from her son's penis (here is a woman in the uncharacteristic role of a circumciser, a mohel), and touched Moses's "feet"—his penis—with it, tricking the homicidal deity into thinking that Moses himself had just been circumcised. What a strange and mysterious God, in this very foreign country.

Not every occurrence of "feet" in the Bible is necessarily euphemistic,[22] as I was reminded when a friend asked me if this sense also applies to the verse "How beautiful on the mountains are the feet of the messenger who proclaims 'Peace.' "[23] On the other hand, when I explain this to students, they often ask about the woman who bathed and kissed the feet of Jesus,[24] and in this case, as both ancient and modern imaginative elaborations suggest, sexual innuendo may be present.

Another word for the genitals is "flesh." Seminal and abnormal discharge from a man's "flesh," and menstrual or other discharge from a woman's "flesh," makes them "unclean" or ritually impure, unable to participate in the community's religious ceremonies. Some words are used exclusively for the male organ; one is "hand." Two different Hebrew words are usually translated "hand." One literally means the forearm, from the tips of the fingers to the elbow;[25] another word refers to what we call the "hand," from the fingertips to the wrist.[26] The former term, because of its resemblance to the erect phallus, is a euphemism for it. A good example of this usage comes from Ugaritic, a second-millennium BCE language closely related to Hebrew. In a Ugaritic myth relating the conception and birth of Dawn and Dusk, "the beautiful and gracious gods," we are told that when the high god El glimpses two women or goddesses,

> El's hand grows as long as the sea
> El's hand [as long] as the ocean.

The same euphemistic sense of "hand" occurs in one of the rules for the community in the Dead Sea Scrolls: "Whoever takes out his hand from under his clothes and his nakedness is seen will be punished for thirty days."[27] It is also found in the Bible. In the book of Isaiah, speaking in the name of the LORD, the prophet condemns Israel, personified as a woman, for worshipping other gods, worship that in prophetic hyperbole had a sexual component:

> Behind the door and door frame you placed your
> dildo
> ...you uncovered yourself and went up and
> spread out your bed,
> You made a covenant with them,
> you loved their bed,
> you gazed on their hand.[28]

The word "dildo" is admittedly jarring. Although it is a good English word—used by writers such as Ben Jonson, Shakespeare, and Auden—it does sound off-color. I have chosen it because I think that is precisely what the prophet wanted to convey: Israel is like a wanton woman. The word also illustrates a problem that translators face. The Hebrew word here can mean either "maleness" (hence "dildo") or "memorial." The invented word "re-member-ance" combines the two meanings and conveys the ambiguity.[29]

All cultures employ euphemisms—polite circumlocutions for sex, bodily functions such as urination and defecation, and death. Biblical writers too were reticent to use precise clinical and anatomical words for sexual acts and organs. Such reticence can also be observed in the later history of the Bible, once it had become a book. For example, an ancient scribe, perhaps troubled by the destination of Joshua's spies, added an explanatory gloss to the words of the king of Jericho to the prostitute Rahab—"the men who went into you, *to your house*"[30]—to make readers less likely to think that the spies had gone to Rahab's house for the usual reason that men visit prostitutes. Translators of the Bible have shown the same prudishness, as when, for example, they translate the prophet Ezekiel's description of the Egyptians as "great of flesh" and "lustful," even though, a few chapters later, the text itself is explicit, describing the Egyptians as having "flesh like the flesh of donkeys and emission like the emission of stallions."[31] We will return to matters of translation repeatedly, because to learn what the Bible means, we must first learn what it meant when it was written, and that begins with the words themselves.

With this background in the use of ordinary words for sexual acts and organs, let us return to the Song of Solomon. In it the female lover describes—or dreams of—her lover coming to her.

> I was asleep, but my heart was awake.
>   Listen—my lover is knocking.
> "Open to me, my sister, my darling,
>   my dove, my perfect one,
>   for my head is full of dew,
>   my locks with the drops of night."
> I have stripped off my robe—
>   how can I get dressed again?

I have washed my feet—
    how can I get them dirty?
My lover thrust his hand through the hole,
    and my insides groaned because of him.
I got up to open to my lover,
    and my hands dripped myrrh,
my fingers, running myrrh,
    on the handles of the bolt.
I opened to my lover....[32]

Whether this is narrative, dream, or fantasy is beside the point: the language is erotic. No wonder that it was sung in taverns in late first-century CE Palestine, a practice that the famous Rabbi Akiva sternly disapproved of. When I was studying in a cloistered Catholic seminary in the early 1960s, Bibles were available for us to read and study, but in many of them the Song of Solomon had been carefully razored out, lest its steamy language become what was called "an occasion of sin."

As a collection of writings produced over centuries, the Bible speaks, even sings, with many voices, in a kind of polyphony, sometimes harmonious, sometimes dissonant. The Song of Solomon is one of the most lyrical and most fascinating of those voices. In the foreign country that is the biblical world, the Song is a garden of earthly delights—full of blossoming lilies, fig trees, grape vines, and henna shrubs, turtledoves, foxes, and gazelles, apples, raisins, and pomegranates, cypresses, cedars, and palm trees—a veritable Eden. And the delights are not just those of nature: it is a place where sex—unmarried sex, sex for its own sake and not just for reproduction—is celebrated. Although it is no feminist tract—the woman has less freedom than the man, and is subject to her brothers' control, as well as to the guardians of morality in her city—in the Song, as nowhere else in the Bible, we hear a woman's voice. It is anomalous in another way too—there is no mention of God under any name.[33]

Yet happily this collection of secular love poems is part of the Bible (probably because Solomon's name had been attached to it), and as we listen to other voices in the Bible's polyphony, we should keep in mind this extraordinary expression of mutual desire.

CHAPTER 2

HE WILL RULE OVER YOU

The Status of Women

God, Adam, and Eve, from *The Mirror of Human Salvation* (French, fifteenth century). In the foreground, God, looking like a pope, gives Adam the command not to eat from the tree of knowledge of good and evil, and in the right background, Adam passes on the command to Eve.

When God created humans, the first chapter of Genesis tells us, "Male and female he created them."[1] The author is referring to the physical differences between males and females—their sexual organs and reproductive functions. In the next two chapters of Genesis, however, another author introduces issues of gender, a cultural rather than a biological category—how society constructs its customs, laws, institutions, and values on the basis of the differences.

The story of Eden in those chapters begins with an idyllic paradise. In the garden, besides trees beautiful to look at and providing nutritious fruits, were two special trees. One was the tree of life, which bestowed immortality; the other was the tree of knowledge of good and evil, whose fruit was not to be eaten. I wonder why, in this garden that the LORD God himself had planted, he put this tree at all if he did not want the man and the woman to touch it. Was this the first in a series of many tests that a deity apparently lacking omniscience would impose on his chosen ones? In any case, the man and the woman disobeyed the divine command. Their punishment was death for them, and for their descendants: they were banished from the garden and no longer had access to the tree of life. For the woman, the punishment also included subservience to the man: "Your desire will be for your man, and he will rule over you."[2] So begins, according to the Bible, the divinely ordained paradigm of the subordination of women.

In the biblical world, as in antiquity more generally (and in some respects today as well), society was overwhelmingly patriarchal. The basic unit was the "house of the father," an extended nuclear family over which the patriarch presided. Descent was traced through the father: men were usually identified as the "son of" their father, as in Joshua son of Nun and Isaiah son of Amoz. Women were similarly identified, at least until marriage, as in Rizpah the daughter of Ai and Esther the daughter of Abihail. After marriage, women could also be identified by their husband, as with Bathsheba the daughter of Eliam, the wife of Uriah, and Jael the wife of Heber.

Descent and inheritance were connected. The bulk of the inheritance passed to the oldest son, so in the genealogies in Genesis, the long lists of "begats," usually only the oldest son is named.

When Seth had lived for one hundred five years, he
fathered Enosh. After he had fathered Enosh, Seth
lived for eight hundred seven years, and he fathered
other sons and daughters. Thus all of Seth's days
were nine hundred twelve years, and he died.[3]

When other sons are important for tracing genealogical connections or for the story line, they may also
be named.

When Terah had lived for seventy years, he fathered
Abram, Nahor, and Haran.[4]

Within this patriarchal framework, women—
daughters, wives, mothers, sisters—were subordinates,
and, like younger sons, are often not mentioned. Even
when they have narrative significance, they are frequently
unnamed: we are never told the names of Noah's wife,
Lot's wife, Jephthah's daughter, Samson's mother, Job's
wife, and many other notable women.

Not only were women subordinates in the family
structure, they were also considered essentially inferior. In theory anything, even anyone, could be offered
to God. But no society that routinely practiced human
sacrifice would long survive, and it was usually prohibited in ancient Israel. So there developed an elaborate
system of substitution in which a person who had been
vowed to God could be redeemed, that is, bought back.
A list gives the following equivalents:[5]

	MALES	FEMALES
over 60 years old	15 shekels of silver	10 shekels of silver
age 20 to 60	50 shekels of silver	30 shekels of silver
age 5 to 20	20 shekels of silver	10 shekels of silver
age 1 month to 5 years	5 shekels of silver	3 shekels of silver

The list is divided into age groups. Newborn infants are not mentioned, because of high neonatal mortality. For the rest, the females are worth less than the males in every group.

This patriarchal bias was also expressed socially. Husbands and fathers had virtually absolute control over their wives and daughters. Sarah refers to her husband as her "lord,"[6] and later Abraham is referred to as her "master."[7] Both of these terms are indicative of the status of the wife: she was under her husband's rule, she was his property, like the donkey that knows its master's feeding trough;[8] the word "master" is frequently used for ownership in the laws concerning property. This status, and Sarah's example, is noted with approval in the New Testament:

> Wives [be] under your husbands' rule.... Thus Sarah obeyed Abraham, calling him her "lord"— and you have become her daughters.[9]

As subordinates, women were subject to their fathers and husbands in all sorts of ways. For example, a religious vow made by a woman was null and void when either her father (if she was unmarried) or her husband disapproved of the vow.[10]

Fathers could also dispose of their daughters. One law provides a shocking example:

> When a man sells his daughter as a slave, she shall not go out as male slaves do. If she is bad in the eyes of her lord, who designated her for himself, then he shall let her be redeemed; he is not autho-rized to sell her to a foreign group, because he has been unfair to her. If he designates her for his son, he shall treat her as with daughters. If he takes for himself another woman, he may not diminish her food, or her clothing, or her sexual rights. And if he does not provide these three things, then she may go out without compensation or payment of silver.[11]

This woman was sold by her father as a slave wife. She was her father's property; now she belongs to her new owner, who may, if he chooses, give her instead to his son. There are restrictions on what the new owner may do, and if he does not treat her fairly, she is free to return to her father's house, without her father having to return the buyer's payment. But essentially the woman is entirely subject to the men in her life, who have the legal right to dispose of her as they wish.

For a woman, marriage was not all that different from being sold as a slave wife. A daughter was given to a prospective husband in return for a bride-price paid to her father. A specific law illustrates this:

> If a man seduces a virgin who is not engaged, and lies with her, he must pay the bride-price for her and she will become his wife. But if the father refuses to give her to him, he shall pay silver corresponding to the bride-price for virgins.[12]

Until she was married, the daughter was her father's property—her reproductive role was under his control. A man who seduced her had to marry her—or, if the father was unwilling to have her marry such a scoundrel, he still had to pay the father the full bride-price for virgins as restitution for his damaged property, his daughter now no longer a virgin.

WIDOWS

Further evidence of women's subordination to men is the status of widows. The most vulnerable members of ancient patriarchal societies were those who had no male protector. These included orphans, meaning children whose fathers had died even if their mothers were still alive, and widows. God is described as "the father of orphans and the protector of widows,"[13] and biblical laws, the Prophets, and other texts repeatedly urge the Israelites to imitate God in caring for these powerless persons.

In biblical narrative, the prophet Elijah is reported

to have multiplied food for a widow and her only son, and then, when the son died, to have restored him to life.[14] Because the Gospel writers used the Jewish scriptures to embellish their accounts of the life of Jesus, like Elijah Jesus is reported to have multiplied food[15] and to have raised to life a widow's only son who had died.[16] In both cases, the situation of the widow without a son was dire, and the prophets' miracles made her less vulnerable.

The story of Ruth, a foreign woman married to an Israelite who had died, shows the steps a woman would take to avoid such vulnerability. At the instigation of her mother-in-law, Naomi, also a widow, Ruth took bold action to ensure that she would be remarried, thus providing the necessary male protector both for herself and for Naomi.

VIRGINITY

Having been sent by his master, Abraham, to find a wife for his son Isaac, after a five-hundred-mile journey north, Abraham's servant arrived at his destination, the city where Nahor, Abraham's brother, lived. At the city's spring—an ancient equivalent of the office watercooler, a place for conversation and gossip—the servant meets Rebekah, Abraham's grand-niece, and Isaac's future wife, as it turns out. She was, the biblical writer tells us, "very beautiful to look at, a virgin, whom no man had known."[17]

Virginity before marriage was prized—a man had a right to expect his wife to be a virgin, and a father had a compelling interest in making sure that she was, for the bride-price for daughters who were virgins was much higher than that for those who were not. The late third-century BCE writer Ben Sira, a traditionalist if not a misogynist, advised:

> A daughter is a treasure that keeps her father awake,
>   and worry about her destroys sleep:
> in her youth, fear that she may be rejected,
>   and when she is married, that she be childless;
> in her virginity, fear that she be defiled,
>   or that she become inseminated in her father's
>   house;
> in her husband's house, fear that she be unfaithful,
>   or when she is married, that she be childless.

He goes on to urge fathers to confine their daughters to the house, never visible from the street, and not to allow them to socialize with married women, probably because they would talk to the virgins about sex.[18]

Jephthah's Virgin Daughter

A prominent virgin in biblical narrative is the daughter of Jephthah. Like other leaders of Israel in the book of Judges, he was an outsider—his mother was a prostitute. Although his father had acknowledged him, like most bastards in history and literature Jephthah had lower status in the family. When his half brothers had grown up, they said to him, "You will not have any inheritance in our father's house, for you are the son of another woman." And they "expelled him"—the same wording is used of divorce, making this a formal, legal act of disinheritance.[19] So the outcast Jephthah became an outlaw, leader of a group of men like him who survived by banditry. In biblical history, this was in the late second millennium BCE, before there was a central government headed by a king. Leadership was regional, in the person of "judges," mainly military leaders. As often happened in this time, an Israelite group was threatened by neighbors: in this case, the Ammonites, who lived east of the Jordan River, were threatening Gilead, a tribe of Israel also east of the Jordan. The elders of Gilead turned for help to Jephthah and his private force. Jephthah retorted, "Are you not the ones who hated me and expelled me from my father's house? Why have you come to me now, when you are having trouble?"[20] Nevertheless, Jephthah agreed to help his compatriots, on the condition that if he were victorious, they would make him their leader. Continuing to show his shrewdness, Jephthah first tried to negotiate with the enemy, but when they refused, he prepared for war. On his way to the battlefield, he vowed to the LORD:

> If you will give the Ammonites into my hand, then whatever comes out of the doors of my house to

meet me when I return in peace from the Ammonites will be Yahweh's, and I will offer it up as a burnt offering.[21]

After a predictably massive defeat of the Ammonites, the victorious Jephthah returned home. Like other women welcoming their victorious heroes, Jephthah's daughter, his only child, came to meet him with music and dance. When he saw her coming, he grieved, because, as he said, "I have opened my mouth to Yahweh, and I cannot go back."

Agreeing that his vow was irrevocable, she asked for one favor before her death: "Let me have two months to wander in the mountains and weep for my virginity, I and my companions." Jephthah agreed, and after two months his daughter returned to her father, who carried out his vow, sacrificing his daughter, "who had never known a man."[22]

Human sacrifice is reported in the Bible on other occasions—mostly by individuals such as the wicked kings Ahaz and Manasseh, by foreigners like the Moabite king Mesha, and by both Israelite and non-Israelite worshippers of gods other than Yahweh. Usually the sacrificial victims were males, as in the case of Hiel, who rebuilt Jericho in the ninth century BCE.

At the cost of Abiram his firstborn son he laid its foundation, and at the cost of Segub his youngest son he set up its gates.[23]

This double foundation sacrifice fulfilled the curse pronounced by Joshua after Jericho's walls fell:

> Cursed before Yahweh be the man who proceeds
> to rebuild this city, Jericho. At the cost of his first-
> born son he will lay its foundation, and at the cost
> of his youngest son he will set up its gates.[24]

The fulfillment of the horrible curse shows how abhorrent human sacrifice was to the Israelites, or at least to the biblical historian.

According to biblical law, every firstborn son, like every firstborn male animal, belonged to Yahweh. But these could be redeemed by substituting a less valuable victim or silver.[25] Biblical writers tendentiously accused their neighbors of practicing child sacrifice, but the Israelites were not permitted to do so—although like other prohibitions this was not always observed.

One exception to the prohibition of human sacrifice is God's command to Abraham to sacrifice his beloved "only son" Isaac, an order that Abraham was willing to carry out.[26] Only at the last moment did God stop the sacrifice, and a providentially provided ram was substituted for a surely terrified Isaac, already tied down on the makeshift altar. Since antiquity, readers have been troubled by the story of "the binding of Isaac," as Jewish tradition calls it. Why did God need to test his faithful servant Abraham, who had done whatever God asked? Why did Abraham not object, as he had earlier, when informed of God's plan to destroy the wicked city of Sodom?[27] The narrative leaves these and other questions unanswered. God, it seems, does what he wants. In Christian myth, God's sacrifice of his own firstborn son, Jesus, who like Isaac carries the wood on which he is to be immolated, is understood as an offering pleasing to his father.[28]

Unlike the sons of Hiel and Abraham, Jephthah's daughter is unnamed: of course, she is a woman—a girl, really. Most horribly, there is no divine intervention, no hapless ram caught in a thicket, and no condemnation of her death. In fact, she herself accepts her death at the hands of her father, a willing victim to a patriarchal god in a patriarchal society. And in biblical traditions, Jephthah is remembered alongside Moses, Aaron, Barak, Samson, Samuel, and David as one of Israel's great heroes,[29] even though he sacrificed his daughter in fulfillment of a rash vow.

Celibacy as an Ideal

Jephthah's daughter's death is tragic. For ancient readers part of the tragedy was that she died a virgin, never having had children. Because the primary role of a woman was as wife and especially mother, we find no evidence in the Hebrew Bible of a positive attitude toward lifelong virginity. "Virgins mourn because they have no husbands,"[30] says an anonymous ancient author—an unmarried childless woman was an unfulfilled woman.

In the Hebrew Bible, virginity is an attribute only of women. We find frequent references to women who have not known a man, but never to a man who has not known a woman. In all the laws concerning marriage and rape, a man's previous sexual history is never an issue, only a woman's. There is evidence for optional celibacy among the Essenes, a Jewish sect that broke with the Temple establishment in Jerusalem in the late second century BCE. Some of them moved to the arid wilderness of Judah just west of the Dead Sea, where they founded a community that lasted until the First Jewish Revolt against Rome in 68 CE. There, like later Christian monastic communities, they devoted themselves to a pure life, which for some meant sexual abstinence. (They are also responsible for the Dead Sea Scrolls, their library, which they hid in caves as the revolt began.) Within Judaism, however, the Essenes are an aberration.

Another aberration is Paul, an observant Jew even after his acceptance of Jesus as Messiah. In his first letter to the Christian community at Corinth in Greece, which has sexual morality as one of its principal topics, Paul commends celibacy:

> I say to the unmarried and to widows that it is better
> for them to remain [unmarried], as I also am. But
> if they cannot exercise self-control, let them marry,
> for it is better to marry than to be inflamed.[31]

Paul's view of marriage is that it is the lesser of two evils—better to have an outlet in marriage for sexual urges than to be promiscuous, but far better not to marry at all. Being married, in his view, caused distress and thus distracted believers from their primary calling.

> The unmarried man is concerned about the affairs of the Lord, how to please the Lord. But the married man is concerned about the affairs of the world, how to please his wife, and he is divided. Likewise, the unmarried woman and the virgin are concerned about the affairs of the Lord, so that they may be holy in body and spirit. But the married woman is concerned about the affairs of the world, how to please her husband.[32]

One reason for this view was a belief that Paul shared with many of the first generation of Christians: that Jesus would return in the near future to complete his messianic mission. So, addressing virgins directly, he tells them:

> Concerning virgins, I have no command of the Lord, but I give my opinion as one who by the Lord's mercy is to be trusted. I think that because of the coming crisis everyone should remain as they are.... For the present form of this world is passing away.[33]

Elsewhere in his letters, Paul occasionally quotes Jesus directly, but on this topic he seems unaware of a saying attributed to Jesus praising those who have "made themselves eunuchs for the kingdom of heaven."[34] Perhaps Paul does not quote it because the words are those of Matthew,[35] who wrote after Paul's death, rather than of Jesus himself. In his personal life Jesus was no ascetic, at least when it came to parties: the Gospels report that he was criticized for enjoying food and drink.[36] In any case, if making oneself a eunuch for the kingdom of heaven is taken literally, as the third-century CE theologian Origen reportedly did, it is a radical precept, one that makes my students shudder when I show them the saying.

So Paul, the bachelor, thought that abstinence and celibacy were the highest ideals, and that sex was to be avoided—because he mistakenly thought that the Second Coming of Jesus was imminent. His view has had profound and largely negative consequences in the history of Western Christianity, especially Roman Catholicism. A look at a comprehensive listing of saints illustrates this: only a minute percentage of the men and women canonized over the centuries were married—the vast majority are virgins and celibate males, and occasionally widows and widowers. The book of Revelation reinforces this negative view about sex. Like Paul, its author, traditionally identified as John, thought that Jesus's return would be soon, and when it happened, the one hundred forty-four thousand saved would be men "who have not defiled themselves with women, for they are virgins."[37]

Another fallout from Paul's views is the requirement in the Roman Catholic Church that clergy be celibate.[38] Coming into force in a series of papal decrees in the eleventh and twelfth centuries, partly to ensure that church property not be bequeathed to a priest's heirs, clerical celibacy was and continues to be rationalized by Paul's assertion that only the unmarried can fully devote themselves to the Lord. Apparently, married church leaders, beginning with Peter and continuing for the next millennium, were less than fully committed Christians.

The Virgin Mary

Although the Gospels of Matthew and Luke have very different accounts of the conception, birth, and early life of Jesus—and the other two Gospels have none at all—they agree that his mother was a virgin. In Luke's Gospel, the story of Mary's conception of Jesus is preceded by another story based on a frequent biblical plot motif: a childless couple whose infertility is ended by divine intervention. Narratives like this show that the son eventually born will have a special role. The couple at the beginning of Luke's Gospel, Zechariah and Elizabeth, are aged, like Abraham and Sarah, but, as with them, a direct divine communication promises that a son will be born—in this case John, to be known as "the Baptist." Like Samson, whose unnamed mother was also infertile, he is to be a Nazirite, under vow not to drink alcoholic beverages, for he is to be consecrated to "make ready a people prepared for the Lord."[39]

The next scene in Luke is the appearance of the angel Gabriel to Mary, who announces to her that she will become pregnant with a son, whom she is to name Jesus, and who "will be great, and called the 'son of the Most High,' and the Lord God will give him the throne of his father David." Mary famously objects, "How can this be, since I have not known a man?" The angel assures her that that is not a problem for God, for whom nothing is impossible: the child to be born will be conceived by the power of the Holy Spirit and will thus be the "son of God." Matthew's version differs in many details—for example, the angel appears to Mary's fiancé, Joseph, not to her, and only after her pregnancy is under way. But the conclusion is the same: her pregnancy is from the Holy Spirit, and the son to be born should be named Jesus.[40]

Joseph himself is speechless in the New Testament. In the Gospels he is the husband of Mary, the father of Jesus and other children, and a carpenter or contractor. In Matthew, the only Gospel in which he appears as a character, Joseph, like his namesake the son of Jacob in Genesis, receives revelations through dreams.[41] He and his family lived in Nazareth, a hamlet of only fifty or so houses, proverbial for its insignificance.[42] Later Christian legend, filling in the blanks left by the Gospel writers, concoct fantastic details: Joseph had been chosen by lot to be Mary's husband, clearly a divine decision; at the time of their wedding he was ninety-two, she fourteen—obviously this was a marriage without sex; and he died some twenty years later, having recognized Jesus as his lord and savior.

So, according to Matthew and Luke, Jesus was born of a virgin. But no other New Testament writers mention this. Paul, the earliest Christian author, speaks of Jesus as "born from David's seed according to the flesh,"[43] meaning that he was a descendant of David through his father. Even Matthew and Luke are inconsistent: when they give Jesus's genealogy, although differing in some details, they agree in establishing his ancestral connection with King David through Joseph, who would have to have been Jesus's father for the genealogical link to be valid. The story of the Virgin Birth thus is best understood in terms of the Old Testament parallels on which it builds: even more remarkable than the birth of a child to a postmenopausal sterile woman like Sarah or Elizabeth is the birth of a child to a virgin. So Jesus is special indeed, and that is the point of the story—or more properly, the myth.

Postbiblical Christian tradition, as it wrestled with how exactly to formulate the belief in Jesus's divinity, chose to follow Matthew's and Luke's narratives of the Virgin Birth, ignoring the other evidence. So, in the fourth century, the Creed of the Council of Nicaea affirmed that Jesus was "born of the Virgin Mary." Not only that, but the delivery of the child did not compromise her virginity—according to several early Christian writers, Jesus was born without rupturing his mother's hymen, like sunlight through a pane of glass as some theologians put it, and Mary remained a consecrated virgin throughout her life. This emphasis on Mary's perpetual virginity further illustrates the negative attitude toward sex that has characterized much of Christian teaching for two millennia. But the doctrine of Mary ever virgin is inconsistent with what the New Testament says. According to Matthew, Joseph "did not know" Mary "until she had given birth to a son."[44] While some (mostly Roman Catholic) scholars argue that this need not necessarily mean that the couple had a normal sex life after Jesus's birth, that interpretation is contradicted by references to the brothers and sisters of Jesus, of whom the Gospels tell us there were at least six. One of them was James, "the brother of the Lord"—the only early Christian to have this title, so it must be more than honorific—who, after his brother's death, assumed leadership of the movement that Jesus had started.[45]

WOMEN'S PUBLIC ROLES

The end of the sad story of Jephthah's daughter is a kind of footnote:

> So it became a rule in Israel that annually the
> daughters of Israel would go out to commemorate

the daughter of Jephthah the Gileadite, four days a year.[46]

This annual ritual, a festival exclusively for women, is not mentioned again in the Bible. Elsewhere we do find occasional references to women participating in public and private ceremonies. Like Jephthah's daughter, women celebrated military victories, including Deborah in the song named for her[47] and the women who danced and sang to the accompaniment of hand drums and three-stringed lutes as they welcomed David when he returned from killing the Philistines.[48] Women could lead songs on other occasions, such as a successful harvest,[49] and also functioned as professional mourners.

In religious ceremonies women participated as musicians as well as worshippers, and they are occasionally reported as assisting at shrines and temples—cooking, weaving, and doing other menial tasks. But they were denied leadership roles. This contrasts with evidence from the rest of the ancient world, where women frequently served as priestesses in the temples of goddesses. In the patriarchal society of ancient Israel, where in theory only one deity was to be worshipped, the priests of that male deity were also males.

Judging from the repeated prohibitions and condemnations of the worship of other gods and goddesses, however, such worship was frequent in ancient Israel.

Sometimes it included the worship of a goddess, such as the "queen of heaven," to whom women as well as men burned incense and poured out drink offerings.[50] Presumably women were also involved in domestic rituals, although we have little information about such ceremonies, mostly because the biblical writers focus on official public ritual.

In other religious activities, women could play a role. One example is necromancy, the practice of consulting the dead. Like the worship of deities other than Yahweh, necromancy was expressly prohibited in biblical law and condemned by the prophets, and so it too must have been fairly widespread. Both men and women functioned as mediums, and capital punishment was prescribed for them as for other forms of sorcery and witchcraft. "Thou shalt not suffer a witch to live" is how the King James Version renders one such law, which provided biblical sanction for the execution of witches in Salem, Massachusetts, and elsewhere.[51]

In the Bible the most famous medium is the unnamed woman of Endor, to whom postbiblical tradition pejoratively gives the title "witch," although that is not how she is characterized. She figures in a narrative about Saul, Israel's first king, toward the end of his reign, when he had been abandoned by God in favor of the younger David. As earlier in his career, Saul was at war with the Philistines, the Israelites' primary enemy in this period. Although he sought divine guidance,

"Yahweh did not answer him" in any of the usual ways of ascertaining the divine purpose—dreams, divination, or prophets. Desperate, and in disguise, at night Saul visited a woman in the town of Endor near the battle-field, who was a "ghost-mistress," a medium.

Saul asked the woman to conjure up a ghost, to bring up from the underworld whomever he wished. At first the woman refused. "You must know," she said, "that Saul has banned necromancers and mediums throughout the land." But Saul, his identity still unknown to her, assured her that she would suffer no punishment. So she agreed, and at Saul's request brought up from the dead the prophet Samuel, who at divine command had anointed Saul king in the first place. When the woman saw Samuel—described as "a god coming up from the under-world…an old man wrapped in a prophet's robe"—she knew that her disguised client was Saul himself. As the narrative continues, Samuel speaks directly to Saul, first complaining about having been disturbed, and then pro-claiming the transfer of Saul's throne to David and predicting Saul's death during the battle with the Philis-tines the next day: "Tomorrow you and your sons will be with me."[52]

Here is a woman on the fringes of organized reli-gion. Remarkably, the prohibitions notwithstanding, her power as a medium is effective: Samuel does come back from the grave to deliver a divinely given message. So, for at least one biblical writer, as for many of his ancient contemporaries, it was possible to communicate with the dead.

There is evidence of women functioning as ritual specialists in other ways as well, especially as prophets. Generalizing about prophecy in ancient Israel in particular, and in the ancient Near East more broadly, is risky, for it was a multifaceted and widespread phenomenon. Some prophets were professionals, trained as apprentices under a master prophet; a few were amateurs. Some were closely attached to royal courts, others operated more independently. Many were men, and many were women.

The Bible names four women prophets, who lived during periods throughout Israel's history. The first is Miriam, the sister of Moses and Aaron, who was recognized as one of the leaders of the Israelites after the Exodus from Egypt. Not only is she called a prophet, but she was also the leader, and perhaps even the author, of the victory song after the Israelites escaped.[53] Together with Aaron, she unsuccessfully tried to challenge Moses's authority,[54] yet she was remembered as one of the key leaders of the Exodus.

> For I brought you up out of the land of Egypt,
>> and I redeemed you from the house of slaves;
>> and I sent before you Moses, Aaron, and
>> Miriam.[55]

The second named woman prophet is Deborah, one of Israel's judges and military leaders after the Exodus, when the Israelites had settled in Canaan; like Miriam, she is credited with a victory song. The third is Huldah, who in the late seventh century BCE mistakenly predicted that King Josiah would have a peaceful death—in fact, he died in battle with the Egyptians.[56] The last is Noadiah, who in the mid-fifth century BCE, along with other unnamed prophets, opposed Nehemiah, the Persian-appointed governor of Judah, when he began repairs of the walls of Jerusalem left in ruins during the Babylonians' capture of the city in 586 BCE.[57]

And there were others, unnamed, such as the wife of the prophet Isaiah, who gave birth to their son Maher-shalal-hash-baz.[58] An earlier generation of mostly male scholars thought that she could not have been a prophet—after all, she was a woman—and that her title was simply something like "Mrs. Prophet," but, given the evidence of women as prophets elsewhere in the Bible as well as in the ancient Near East, there is no reason to deny her status as a prophet in her own right. Who knows—perhaps she and her husband had met at prophet school. Other passing references to unnamed women prophets show that this was an activity in which women could play a significant role.[59]

The same is true of women who are called "wise." Two such women, both unnamed, are mentioned in connection with King David. The first, from the village of Tekoa, some ten miles south of Jerusalem, was brought to David by his general Joab as part of Joab's plan to have David allow his son Absalom to return to the court. (Absalom had been banished for having murdered his half brother Amnon, who had raped Absalom's full sister Tamar.) The Tekoa woman apparently was a gifted storyteller, able to persuade David to rule in a fictional case for which Joab provided the script. Presenting herself as a widow, she tells the king that one of her two sons had killed the other, and now the clan wants to execute the murderer, her only surviving son, as punishment. This, she pleads, would leave her bereft. David decides for the woman and promises royal amnesty for the son. The woman then draws the parallel, as Joab had intended: Absalom should also be pardoned, and David agrees.[60] What the woman's "wisdom" consists of is not stated—perhaps it is her storytelling skill.

Later in David's reign, during a revolt by Sheba from the tribe of Benjamin against David's rule, Joab and the army pursued the rebel to the northern city of Abel, where he had holed up. With the city under siege, another unnamed wise woman successfully negotiated with Joab to save her city. She persuaded her fellow citizens to toss the rebel's head from the city wall to Joab, and the city was saved.[61]

These women are both characterized as wise, and undoubtedly there were others like them in ancient Israel—women whose savvy and sense enabled them to achieve some distinction in their towns. But ultimately they still remained subject to patriarchal authorities.

The tradition of women prophets continued in post-biblical Judaism and in early Christianity. The Gospel of Luke mentions Anna, an aged widow and also a prophet, who blessed Jesus shortly after his birth. Unlike her male counterpart, Simeon, however, the words of her blessing are not given, nor are we told that she was inspired by the Holy Spirit, as he was.[62] Other New Testament books make passing reference to women prophets, including four unnamed virgin daughters of the early Christian leader Philip,[63] and women whose prophesying was part of early Christian ritual.[64] But of the content of their prophecies we are told nothing.

Because of ancient Israel's patriarchal structure, women seldom held high public office. In the premonarchic era, the period of the judges in the late second millennium BCE, the only exception is Deborah, who is described both as a judge and also as a kind of co-general with her male counterpart, Barak, in a battle with the Canaanites.[65] After the battle, Jael with her deadly tent peg killed the Canaanite general Sisera,[66] much as in later Jewish fiction the pious widow Judith would kill the Assyrian general Holofernes after seducing him.[67] But both Jael and Judith used feminine wiles to achieve their ends, and they did not hold official positions.

During the period of the monarchy, the first half of the first millennium BCE, both queens and queen mothers had authority, derived from their position as wife of the ruling monarch and, after their husband's death, as mother of his successor. Jezebel, the notorious Phoenician wife of King Ahab of the northern kingdom of Israel in the ninth century BCE, acted without her husband's knowledge in expropriating a vineyard that her husband wanted, adjacent to one of their palaces. But she did so in his name, in documents sealed with his seal, falsely accusing Naboth, the vineyard's owner, of blasphemy and treason. Naboth was found guilty of the trumped-up charge and executed as the law required; his vineyard was then seized by eminent domain. For this heinous violation of Israelite law, both Jezebel and Ahab were condemned by the prophet Elijah, who predicted their violent deaths as divinely imposed punishment.[68]

The foreigner Jezebel brought with her into the Israelite court at Samaria the worship of her native deities—including, we are told, hundreds of prophets of the god Baal and the goddess Asherah, for which she is also condemned.[69] Similar apostasy is reported about other queens and queen mothers. In the early ninth century BCE, the Judean king Asa removed his mother, Maacah, from her position as queen mother because she had made a "horrid object"—perhaps a statue or phallic image—for Asherah.[70] Worship of gods other than Yahweh is also reported of Athaliah, Ahab's (and probably Jezebel's) daughter, who had been married to Jehoram, king of Judah in the mid-ninth century BCE. After the deaths of her husband and his successor, their son Ahaziah, Athaliah was sole ruler of Judah, the only woman in ancient Israel who was head of state. That lasted six years, until she was killed in a coup led by the high priest in the Temple of Yahweh. He may have done so to eliminate a rival temple of Baal in Jerusalem that was under Athaliah's patronage.[71]

With few exceptions, then, women did not exercise power independently in ancient Israel. That continued in subsequent Judaism, until recently. The priesthood, and later the rabbinate, was reserved exclusively for men. There is scattered evidence that in some Jewish communities in the Diaspora in the Roman period women were local leaders—particularly elders and heads of synagogues—but that was also exceptional, and eventually ceased. Not until the late twentieth century would first Reform Jews and then Reconstructionist and Conservative Jews ordain women as rabbis.

We find the same picture in earliest Christianity. The norm is male leadership, although there are exceptions, usually in passing references in the New Testament, as in the greetings that conclude many of Paul's letters. One of these mentions "Nympha and the church in her house."[72] Here is a woman wealthy enough to have a local Christian assembly ("the church") in the city of Colossae in western Asia Minor gather for regular weekly meetings at her home. Was she a widow, or a convert to Christianity but her husband was not? No details are given. Another is Junia, mentioned by Paul at the close of his letter to the

Romans as someone who was "prominent among the apostles."[73] The title "apostle" here does not refer to "the Twelve," Jesus's inner circle; it is used more broadly in the sense of "ambassador" for Christ, as it was for Paul, Barnabas, Apollos, and others who did not belong to the Twelve. Junia was an apostle in this latter sense, a notion so inconceivable to male interpreters and translators that until the late twentieth century she was usually given a sex change: her name was interpreted as a man's name, Junias, so that this only woman apostle of whom we know was in effect excised from history. Perhaps similar to Junia were Euodia and Syntyche, mentioned in another of Paul's letters as having struggled alongside him in his work of spreading the gospel.[74]

Then there is Phoebe, who was a deacon.[75] The Greek word *diakonos* literally means "minister," in the sense of one who attended to the material needs of the community, like the seven men, traditionally called "deacons," chosen by the Twelve after Jesus's death to oversee the distribution of food in the church in Jerusalem.[76] Phoebe is also called a "benefactor." She was apparently another wealthy woman who provided for the needs of her church, much as there were wealthy women who "ministered" to Jesus and the Twelve out of their own resources.[77] For the most part, however, as in contemporaneous Judaism, the leaders of the early Christian movement were men.

WOMEN'S DOMESTIC ROLES

The book of Proverbs, a collection of both popular and learned reflections on the human condition, concludes with a lengthy poetic portrait of the ideal wife. The poem begins by identifying her as "a woman of power" or "a powerful woman." A more usual translation is "a capable wife" or "a virtuous woman," but the original Hebrew phrase includes a word that really means "might" or "power," and it is often used in this sense of warriors and heroes—the patriarchalism of translators obscures the remarkable attribution of strength and power to the model Israelite woman. The poem is an acrostic, one of more than a dozen in the Bible, in which the first verse begins with the first letter of the alphabet, and each successive line with the next letter. This device gives the poem a formal unity, making up for a lack of logical development. Instead, the poet almost randomly describes, from A to Z (as it were), the qualities of a woman who is an energetic and resourceful provider for her family, a wise teacher, and a patron of the poor.

> Who can find a woman of power?
> > Her worth is far more precious than coral jewels.
> Her husband's heart trusts in her;
> > he will not lack wealth.
> She provides him with good, not evil,
> > all the days of her life.
> She looks for wool and flax,

and her hands take pleasure in being busy.
She is like a merchant fleet:
    she imports her food from afar.
She gets up when it is still night,
    and provides provisions for her house,
    and gives orders to her maidservants.
She inspects a field and buys it;
    with the fruit of her hands she plants a vineyard.
She girds her loins with might,
    and strengthens her arms.
She senses that trade is good,
    and her lamp does not go out at night.
She puts her arms to the distaff,
    and her hands hold the spindle.
She stretches out her hand to the poor,
    and extends her arms to the needy.
She does not fear for her household because of snow,
    because her entire household is clothed in scarlet.
She makes covers for herself;
    her clothing is linen and purple.
Her husband is known in the gates,
    when he sits with the elders of the land.
She makes a garment and sells it,
    and she gives her sashes to the Canaanite
        merchant.
Might and splendor are her clothing,
    and she laughs at what is to come.
She opens her mouth with wisdom,
    and instruction to be kind is on her tongue.
She watches over the ways of her household,
    and does not eat bread of idleness.

Her sons get up and call her blessed;
    her husband likewise praises her:
"Many women have acted powerfully,
    but you surpass all of them."
Charm is deceptive and beauty evanescent:
    a woman who fears the LORD is to be praised.
Give her credit for the fruit of her hands,
    and her works will bring her praise in the gates.[78]

This is indeed a remarkable woman, but also one constrained by the patriarchal structure. She apparently has some delegated authority to buy land and to engage in commerce, but it is in a man's world. She works from before dawn until well into the night, while her husband sits at the city gates, where men gathered as they still do in Middle Eastern cafés, and basks in the fame she has brought him.

This ideal wife is the object of the poet's attention, but she never speaks: he watches from afar but never gets inside her head or heart. This unique poem, with its window into how women functioned in Israelite society, may in fact be a kind of manual or guide for young women about to be married—in essence, a short course in home economics.

Within the patriarchal structure, then, a wife and mother had some authority. "Honor your father and your mother," says the commandment.[79] If it said simply, "Honor your father," we would not be surprised, but the inclusion of the mother shows that she had some status.

In biblical narrative we also meet women who exercised initiative within the patriarchal structure, such as Abigail. When David was on the run from Saul, he had his own band of fighters who supported themselves by being mercenaries and, like Jephthah's men, by banditry and by a kind of protection racket. According to 1 Samuel 25, David heard that a wealthy man in his territory, Nabal (whose name means "fool"), was shearing his three thousand sheep. David sent some of his men with a message:

> Peace be to you, and peace be to your house, and peace be to all that is yours! I have heard that you are shearing now. Your shepherds were with us in the wilderness, and we did not harm them, nor did they miss anything all the time they were in Carmel—ask your servants, and they will tell you! So now, let my servants find favor in your eyes, because we have come on a holiday. Give whatever you can find to your servants and to your son David.

Nabal, earlier described as stingy and rude, angrily refused to give anything to "these men who came from I do not know where" and sent them off empty-handed. David told his men to prepare for a raid.

But when Abigail, Nabal's wife, heard what had happened, she "quickly took two hundred loaves of bread, two skins of wine, five dressed sheep, a bushel of parched grain, two quarts of raisins, and two hundred cakes of figs" and brought them personally to David, whom she encountered as he was preparing to attack. Her bribe worked, and David relented. The next morning, when Nabal was sober (he had been partying with the sheep-shearers), Abigail told him what she had done, and he suffered a massive stroke and died ten days later. When David heard of the foolish Nabal's death, he sent a message to Abigail that he wanted to take her as his own wife (his third, in fact), an offer she quickly accepted, knowing, as did other Israelites, of David's ambition to become king.[80]

For David, like tribal leaders in other cultures, it was a calculated marriage, giving him a secure base and following in the land that he would eventually rule. Abigail is a paragon: beautiful and smart, but also calculating. She successfully exploited the patriarchal system—first to save herself and her kin and then to improve her standing. But it was all within the context of that system.

Until the mid-twentieth century, biblical scholarship had its own kind of patriarchy: it was almost entirely a male profession. In the early days of feminist biblical scholarship, from the 1960s to the 1980s, in line with the developing feminist movement, women and a few men began to take a fresh look at biblical traditions. They discovered in them evidence that mitigated the overwhelmingly patriarchal bias of the Bible. In particular, they suggested that in some periods women did achieve a kind of equality with men.

In the period of the judges, between the Israelites' Exodus from Egypt in the thirteenth century and the establishment of the monarchy in the late tenth century BCE, some argued, gender roles in Israel were less fixed, so that women could hold positions of political and military leadership, as Deborah did. Likewise, in the first decades of Christianity, some scholars suggested, women also had a measure of equality, following the inclusive example of Jesus. In Christ Jesus, wrote Paul, "there is not Jew or Greek, there is not slave or free, there is not male and female."[81] Scholars pointed to the presence of women among Jesus's followers and the identification of some women as holding the offices of deacon and even apostle. These were, some scholars argued, the authentic biblical traditions, and they gave both authority and comfort to modern women striving for equality in their communities of faith.

But more recently, those we may call "postfeminists" have been taking another look. Although there were women in biblical times who attained some positions of authority, they were relatively few. Ben Sira includes in his catalog of heroes of Israel's history only "famous men,"[82] as would almost every such catalog in any culture before the mid-twentieth century. Also symptomatic is the fact that of the approximately thirty-eight books of the Hebrew Bible, only two, Ruth and Esther, have women's names as titles, and not one is traditionally ascribed to a woman author. And of the twenty-seven books of the New Testament, none have either a woman's name as title or a woman author.

Even though Jesus did include women among his followers, and apparently associated with them more freely than was the social norm of his day, there still were no women among the Twelve, his inner circle, nor are any mentioned as present at the Last Supper. And while some women did have leadership roles in the scattered communities of Christianity in the mid-first century, as they also did in some Jewish communities, this was not the norm. In any case it soon tapered off. Paul's words, "in Christ Jesus...no male and female," have more recently been interpreted not as a ringing affirmation of gender equality but as a slogan restating his deep opposition to both sex and marriage.

Certainly Paul was no feminist:

> As in all the churches of the saints, women should be silent in the churches. For it is not allowed to them to speak, but they should be subordinate, as the Law also says. If they wish to learn something, let them ask their husbands at home. For it is shameful for a woman to speak in church.[83]

This admonition is so chauvinistic that some scholars think that they may not be Paul's own words—wishful thinking, in my view. To be sure, Paul is not entirely consistent in the letters he wrote over the course of a decade or more, but these verses are found in every ancient manuscript of the New Testament. A later writer who used Paul's name expressed similar sentiments:

> Let a woman learn in silence, with full submission. I allow no woman to teach or to have authority over a man. For Adam was formed first, then Eve. And Adam was not deceived, but the woman, deceived, committed transgression.[84]

All of these words are part of canonical and authoritative scripture for Christians, and as such were followed by all Christians until the nineteenth century, and still are by some.

As a last example from the New Testament, consider the women who discovered Jesus's empty tomb. According to all four Gospels, on the Sunday morning after Jesus's execution one or more women went to the tomb where he had been buried and found it empty.[85] Early feminist scholars saw this as paradigmatic: women were the first to be given the good news that Jesus had been raised from the dead, and they became the first evangelists, spreading that good news, that gospel. Postfeminist interpretation, however, has a different spin. Why had the women gone to the tomb? To complete the burial preparations for Jesus's body, a women's task that had been interrupted by the Sabbath, when such activity would not have been allowed. Moreover, they did not really spread the news far and wide. Rather, following angelic instructions, they reported their discovery to Jesus's male disciples, Peter and the rest of the eleven (Judas having committed suicide a few days before). So the women were in effect simply messengers to the male authorities, who scarcely acknowledged their role.

Here is how Paul describes the chain of tradition about the appearances of Jesus after he had been raised:

> First and foremost I handed on to you what I received, that Christ...was raised on the third day according to the scriptures, and that he was seen by Peter, then by the Twelve. After that he was seen by more than five hundred brothers at one time, of whom most are still alive, although some have fallen asleep. Then he was seen by James, and then by all the apostles.[86]

Even if the terms "brothers" and "apostles" are inclusive, referring to both women and men, in his catalog of those who had seen Jesus Paul mentions no women explicitly, not even those who had discovered the empty tomb. Nor, significantly perhaps, does he even mention the empty tomb, which may have been a myth developed after his time.

Were there differences in the treatment of gender in the more than a thousand years depicted in the Bible's pages? Some, to be sure—for example, the curse in the Eden story is reversed in the Song of Solomon, when the woman says, "I am my lover's, and his desire is for me."[87]

But the dominant paradigm, both in the various biblical sources and over the centuries, is static: the consistent picture we get for ancient Israel, early Judaism, and early Christianity is patriarchal. The first woman was punished for her disobedience by the divine decree that her husband would rule over her, and that applied to her descendants as well, just as the punishment of hard work and ultimately death applied not only to the first man but to all subsequent generations.[88] That decree illustrates the bleakness of the overall biblical picture for feminists who would claim the Bible as an authority.

Unfortunately, the Bible's pervasive patriarchal bias has been selectively utilized by past and present religious leaders, who find in the Bible license, even authorization, for the subordination of women. Every morning, observant Jewish men say this prayer: "Blessed art thou, O Lord our God, king of the universe, who has not made me a woman." This reflects a correct understanding of biblical views of the superiority of men to women, as does Paul's paraphrase of the creation story, that the woman was created for the sake of the man, and therefore the husband is the head of the wife.[89] If there were women who achieved positions of authority, that was exceptional rather than usual.

After six decades as a member of the Southern Baptist Convention, former President Jimmy Carter announced in 2009 that he was leaving it. He did so because of the church's insistence that women are inferior to men and should be subservient to them—after all, the Bible says so. But for Carter, this is clearly a violation of the teachings of Moses and the prophets, Jesus, Paul, Muhammad, and founders of other religions. Carter overstates his case, but in essence he is appealing to a higher principle underlying the specific texts of scripture that clearly reinforce men's domination of women. Those texts, he correctly recognizes, "owe more to time and place—and the determination of male leaders to hold onto their influence—than eternal truths."[90]

CHAPTER 3

AS IT WAS IN THE BEGINNING?

Marriage and Divorce

Matthias Stomer (ca. 1600–1652), *Sarah Bringing Hagar to Abraham.*

I am sometimes asked by relatives and students to suggest biblical passages for use at their weddings, but few
are appropriate. The Song of Solomon is too erotic—
not to mention that the lovers are not married. Most
texts concerning married couples are permeated with
patriarchalism. Many major biblical characters had more
than one wife. Because biblical views on marriage origi-
nated in societies whose mores were in many ways different from ours, biblical models do not necessarily inform
either our practice or our theory of marriage. As a result,
couples seeking my advice usually end up choosing Paul's
vague if eloquent catalog of the qualities of love—"love
is patient, love is kind," and so on[1]—which is not about
marriage at all but about the greatest of spiritual gifts.

In our culture, marriage is closely connected with the
idea of romance. Two persons "fall in love," and after some

exploration of their compatibility, decide to wed. This was not the pattern in ancient times, notably in the biblical world—a foreign country not just in its language but also in its social institutions. A deep probe into biblical views of marriage and divorce helps us learn more about issues of gender and the status of women in biblical times.

The primary function of marriage was to produce offspring—especially, as in most patriarchal societies, male offspring. According to the psalmists,

> Sons are an inheritance from Yahweh,
>   the fruit of the womb a reward;
> like arrows in the hand of a warrior
>   so are the sons of one's youth:
> Happy is the man
>   who has filled his quiver with them.[2]

> Your wife shall be like a fruitful vine
>   in the interior of your house,
> Your sons like olive shoots
>   surrounding your table....
> May you see your sons' sons.[3]

ABORTION

Because children were a valuable economic asset, and because infant mortality was high—as much as fifty percent—the ancient Israelites did not usually practice birth control.[4] In particular, abortion as a means of birth control is not mentioned anywhere in the Hebrew

Bible, or in the New Testament.[5] That absence of evidence has not prevented both sides in the ongoing debate about abortion from citing the Bible in support of their respective positions. Pro-choice advocates often refer to the following law:

> When men are fighting and strike a pregnant woman so that her child comes out but there is no harm, then he should be fined as the woman's husband shall specify, and he should give a fair assessment. But if there is harm, then you should give life for life, eye for eye, tooth for tooth, hand for hand, foot for foot, burn for burn, wound for wound, bruise for bruise.[6]

The general rule is the famous "law of talion"—"eye for eye, tooth for tooth"—the principle that the punishment fits the crime.[7] In this case, a pregnant woman tries to break up a fight between her husband and another man. In the melee her husband's opponent strikes her so that she miscarries. The law states that if that is the only damage, he must pay a fine. But if there is injury, presumably to the wife, then the punishment corresponds to the harm done. The pro-choice argument is that the "life for life" principle clearly does not apply to the fetus, and therefore the fetus was not considered a human person; otherwise, the loss of its "life" would require the assailant's death rather than just a fine. "Thou shalt not kill" is thus irrelevant when it comes to abortion.

One of the atrocities of war, both ancient and

modern, is ripping open pregnant women. Although generally condemned in the Bible,[8] in one passage it is included along with killing of infants as a component of the divine judgment that will fall on Samaria, the capital of the northern kingdom, for its guilt.[9] Whether the punishment was actually to be carried out by invading enemies is beside the point: in the prophet's interpretation they were acting as divine agents. The prophet proclaims that the punishment is divinely imposed. Does that make God an abortionist? Perhaps so—he certainly is in the difficult case of a woman whose husband suspects that she has been unfaithful, possibly because she is pregnant. She is subjected to a mysterious ritual ordeal in which, if she is guilty, the LORD will cause her to abort the fetus.[10]

Opponents of abortion, undeterred by its lack of mention in the Bible, find support for their view that the fetus is a human person in texts that describe divine providence in caring for a person even before birth. Words put in Job's mouth are representative. Speaking of his servants (or slaves), he says:

> Did not the one who made me in the belly make them,
> the same one fashion us in the womb?[11]

Other texts similarly attribute prenatal development to divine intent. Earlier Job had addressed God, complaining that what God had recently done to him made no sense:

Your hands shaped me and made me,
> But now you have turned and have swallowed
> me up.
Remember that like clay you made me:
> Would you now return me to the dust?
Did you not pour me out like milk,
> curdle me like cheese?
With skin and flesh you clothed me,
> and wove me together with bones and tendons....
Why did you bring me out of the womb?[12]

This and related texts, not scientific by our standards, do reflect in a naïve, even sentimental way individuals' retrospective understanding of how providence was responsible for their existence. But they are hardly clear statements about the status of the fetus as a human person. Moreover, this understanding of providence fails to explain the high rate of prenatal mortality: if God is so concerned about every fetus, then why are there so many miscarriages? The modern question about the status of the fetus was not one that concerned the biblical writers, and the little they have to say about it is not consistent.

ARRANGED MARRIAGES

As in some cultures today, marriages were arranged. The usual pattern was for the male heads of household of the prospective husband and wife to act as principals. This is the case with Isaac and Rebekah, whose marriage was arranged by a servant of Isaac's father, Abraham, with

Rebekah's brother, Laban, and her father, Bethuel.[13] As instructed, the servant traveled some five hundred miles from southern Canaan to Aram-naharaim in what is now northern Syria to procure a wife for Isaac from Abraham's kin—his "father's house"—back in the land he had left at divine command. After lengthy negotiation and the presentation of lavish gifts, presumably including the bride-price, Rebekah's parents, her brother, and Rebekah herself all consented to the marriage. Rebekah then left her family and traveled south with the servant to Abraham's home.[14] Similarly, a proposed marriage between Dinah, the daughter of Jacob, and Shechem, the son of Hamor, was negotiated by the two fathers, along with Shechem and Jacob's sons.[15]

Jacob, Moses, and David as prospective husbands negotiated directly with the fathers of their brides-to-be.[16] But both Jacob and Moses were fugitives, distant from their homeland and thus from their parents, who would not have been in a position to conduct the negotiations. David's situation is analogous: he had left his family and joined the army of King Saul. In the king's service, David was so successful that Saul became jealous. Plotting to have David killed, Saul offered him his daughter Michal as a wife, and set the bride-price: one hundred Philistine foreskins. Saul did not want them—he wanted David dead. But David foiled his plan. Like a true hero he brought back twice as many, and so Saul, reluctantly, had to give him Michal, who became David's first wife.

Sometimes the bride-price could be paid through labor. Jacob had no resources of his own, because he had fled from his angry older brother, Esau, and gone to get a wife from the family of his uncle, Laban. He contracted to work for Laban for seven years in order to marry Laban's younger daughter, Rachel, Jacob's first cousin. At the wedding, Laban substituted his older daughter, Leah, for Rachel. Because the bride was veiled,[17] Jacob was unaware of the substitution until the following morning, when the marriage had been consummated. So Jacob worked another seven years for Rachel, his first choice. Usually, however, the bride-price was something of value. The prophet Hosea, we are told, purchased his wife for fifteen shekels (about six ounces) of silver, a homer (about six and a half bushels) of barley, and a large jar of wine.[18] This would make her value roughly the same as that of a woman elsewhere, about thirty shekels of silver.[19]

Marriage was a contract—the Hebrew word is *berît,* used mostly for the contract or covenant between God and Israel—between a man and the father of the bride-to-be, and also between husband and wife.[20] The marriage contract had two stages. The first was the engagement or betrothal, in which a woman—usually a young girl just past puberty—was legally transferred from her father to her husband-to-be. After this, even before the actual wedding, the woman was her fiancé's property, and a man who raped her was guilty of adultery.[21] Then, after an interval that varied, the wedding took place and the marriage was consummated. We still have vestiges of this ancient patriarchalism. At many American weddings, the bride is "given away" by her father, and not so long ago a prospective husband would ask his intended's father for "her hand in marriage," a practice that now seems quaint.

ENDOGAMY AND EXOGAMY

An important factor in the choice of the bride was that she belong to the same ethnic (and therefore religious) group. Known as endogamy, this ensured both that the group and its traditions would survive and also that property would stay within the group. The principle is stated explicitly in the book of Tobit, where its hero, Tobit, instructs his son Tobias:

> First of all, take a wife from the seed of your fathers; do not take a foreign wife, who is not of your father's tribe; for we are the sons of the prophets. Remember, my son, that Noah, Abraham, Isaac, and Jacob, our ancestors of old, all took wives from among their kindred. They were blessed in their children, and their seed will inherit the land.[22]

In accord with this principle, Ishmael, Abraham's son through Hagar the Egyptian, had an Egyptian wife, in a marriage arranged by his mother after she had been forced out of the household: he married one of his mother's group.[23] Jacob's older but unchosen brother, Esau, had married two Hittite women, but Jacob was instructed by his father, Isaac:

> Go to Paddan-aram, to the house of Bethuel, your mother's father, and take as a wife for yourself from there one of the daughters of Laban, your mother's brother.[24]

This resulted in complicated interrelationships: Isaac married his uncle's granddaughter, Jacob married his cousins Leah and Rachel, and one of Esau's wives was his cousin Mahalath.

We find an explicit reason for endogamy in biblical law, in the context of the Israelites' relationships with the inhabitants of the Promised Land:

> You should not intermarry with them. You should not give your daughter to his son, nor shall you take his daughter for your son, for that would turn away your son from me to serve other gods.[25]

An illustration of how marriage outside the group, or exogamy, could compromise a group's religious traditions is the infamous Jezebel, the daughter of the king of Tyre, who was married to Ahab, king of Israel. To the Israelite court she brought her own deities, Baal and Asherah, and their prophets, hundreds of them, and it was those deities whom she incited her husband to worship.[26]

Mixed marriage was opposed, then, because it would, and still does, result in dilution of a group's identity, both ethnic and religious. Just consider *Abie's Irish Rose, Guess Who's Coming to Dinner, Meet the Parents,* or any number of American experiences of exogamous marriage.

Yet not surprisingly, given its composite nature, the Bible also refers to exogamy without criticism and sometimes even with praise. Notable examples include the patriarch Judah, who married a Canaanite;[27] Joseph in Egypt, who, having gone native himself, not surprisingly married an Egyptian woman;[28] and Boaz, an Israelite who married Ruth, a Moabite woman, who would become King David's great-grandmother.[29] Even Moses married outside the group,[30] which became a matter of family controversy when Aaron and Miriam, his brother and sister, tried to wrest the leadership away from him.[31]

Another person in a mixed marriage was Esther, identified in the book named for her as one of many wives of the king of Persia in the fifth century BCE. Different versions of her story provide further evidence of the Bible's inconsistency about endogamy. The traditional Hebrew version of the book of Esther is a novella, a short fiction, and is a fully secular work. In it God is never mentioned, Esther's Jewishness is ethnic rather than religious, and her inclusion in the king's harem is unnoteworthy. In the ancient Near East, however, a book was often something more fluid than our traditional view of a work written by a single author, produced, published, and never altered. Not only was a book usually unsigned, so its author often was unknown, but a book could also become a kind of hypertext, which subsequent writers could change as they chose. Such fluidity exists in the books of Jeremiah, Job, Ezra, and Daniel; in the Gospels of Mark and John in the New Testament; and also in the book of Esther. In addition to the traditional version of Esther, there is another, preserved only in Greek, that gives a very different picture. In this bowdlerized revision, God is mentioned more than fifty times, and Esther's situation in the royal court is repulsive to her. When she prays to God for help, she claims:

> You know how I hate the glory of the lawless and loathe the bed of the uncircumcised and of every foreigner.[32]

For the revisers of the original text of the book of Esther, her marriage to the Gentile king of Persia was abhorrent if unavoidable. So the history of the book of Esther itself is further evidence of an ambivalent attitude toward exogamy in biblical times.

POLYGAMY

Once upon a time, the Bible relates on several occasions, there lived a man whose wife was infertile—"barren," in the traditional and infelicitous and pejorative translation. What was he to do, what were they to do in this situation, given the importance of having offspring, especially sons? In some cases, God intervened, as with Samson's father, Manoah, and his unnamed mother;[33] Samuel's mother, Hannah;[34] John the Baptist's parents, Zechariah and Elizabeth;[35] and others. But the couple could also be proactive, as with Abram (later called Abraham) and Sarai (later called Sarah).

> Now Sarai, Abram's wife, had not borne children
> for him. She had an Egyptian slave, whose name
> was Hagar. Sarai said to Abram, "Because Yahweh
> has prevented me from bearing children, go into
> my slave; perhaps I may be built up by her." Abram
> listened to Sarai. So Sarai, Abram's wife, took
> Hagar her Egyptian slave...and she gave her to
> Abram her husband as a wife. So Abram went into
> Hagar and she became pregnant.[36]

At this point, the happy extended family ruptured: when Hagar treated Sarai with contempt, Sarai forced her to leave, without objection from Abram.[37] But Hagar was divinely protected, and in due time she gave birth to Ishmael.

God had repeatedly promised Abram that he would father a multitude of offspring, more numerous than the stars in the sky or the particles of soil in the ground. But Sarai was postmenopausal, some ninety years old, and Abram was a hundred. (That is why she gave Hagar to her husband, so that she could be a mother through her slave.) But God's promise was not to be fulfilled through Ishmael. One hot summer day, Abraham (as he is now called) was sitting, as modern Bedouin still do, at the entrance of his tent, which was pitched near a large terebinth, one of those stately trees that dot southern Judah. Three men on foot approached him, and Abraham welcomed them with typical nomadic hospitality: a full meal of freshly baked flatbread, meat from a calf slaughtered for the occasion, and milk and yogurt. During the meal, which must have taken some time to prepare, one of the visitors asked Abraham, "Where is Sarah, your wife?" and he replied that she was inside the tent, where, the narrator tells us, she was listening to the conversation. One of the visitors then said, "I will return to you next year, and Sarah your wife will have a son."[38] Abraham by now must have realized what we readers have already been told, that one of his visitors was Yahweh himself, dropping in for dinner as deities sometimes do.

The divine promise was kept, and Sarah became pregnant and gave birth to a son, named Isaac. Let me digress here about Isaac's name, returning to issues of euphemism and innuendo. The root meaning of Isaac's name is "laughter," reiterated in the narratives about the promise of his conception and of his birth. When Sarah overheard the divine promise, she

> laughed to herself, saying: "After I am worn out, shall I have pleasure? And my lord is old!" And

Yahweh said to Abraham, "Why did Sarah laugh, and say, 'Shall I really bear a child, even though I am old?' Is anything too wonderful for Yahweh?"...But Sarah lied, and said, "I did not laugh," because she was afraid. But he said, "Yes, you did laugh."[39]

Then, when Isaac was born, Sarah exclaimed, "God has brought laughter for me, because whoever hears of this will laugh with me."[40]

The same word is used in two other stories about Isaac. Many years later, Isaac found himself an alien, a stranger in a foreign land, just like his father, Abraham, twice before. This time, Isaac is in Philistine territory between Gaza and Beer-sheba, with his beautiful wife, Rebekah. When the locals asked him about his wife, like Abraham he said,

> "She is my sister," because he was afraid to say, "She is my wife," [thinking,] "the men of the place might kill me on account of Rebekah, because she is beautiful."

Then,

> after he had been there for some time, Abimelech, the king of the Philistines, looked out a window and saw Isaac making his wife Rebekah laugh. So Abimelech summoned Isaac, and said: "She is your wife!"[41]

Here "laugh" must have a sexual connotation, as modern translations implicitly recognize when they have Isaac "sporting with," "fondling," or "caressing" Rebekah;[42] only one comes close to both the literal and the suggestive meanings, when it has Abimelech seeing "Isaac and his wife Rebekah laughing together."[43] In any case, the sense is clear: whatever exactly Isaac and Rebekah were doing was sexual, not how a brother and sister normally act.[44]

The same sense occurs in a story set early in Isaac's life. After Isaac had been weaned, Abraham threw a big party to celebrate the survival of this boy beyond infancy, with its considerable risks. During the party,

> Sarah saw the son of Hagar the Egyptian, whom she had borne to Abraham, making her son Isaac laugh. And she said to Abraham, "Expel this slave woman and her son—for this slave woman's son will not inherit with my son Isaac."[45]

What was Ishmael doing? The intent of the narrator is to suggest something awful: Ishmael was "playing with" Isaac: that—as well as not wanting Isaac's inheritance to be diminished—is why Sarah had Abraham send Ishmael and Hagar away. There is a hint of homosexual incest here, an example of scurrilous attribution of unacceptable sexual behavior to others—in the Bible, non-Israelites.

Back now to polygamy. In the Jacob narrative there are more examples of a childless wife giving her slave to her husband in order to provide her husband with children through her—a kind of ancient equivalent of surrogate mothering. Rachel gives her slave Bilhah to Jacob, and only then, like Sarah, is she able to have children; likewise, Rachel's sister Leah, Jacob's first wife, gives her slave Zilpah to Jacob for a similar reason.[46]

As these narratives illustrate, polygamy—or more properly polygyny, the practice of a man having more than one wife—was acceptable in ancient Israel. In addition to Sarah and Hagar, Abraham had another wife, Keturah, who also bore him six sons, in the favored multiples of six found throughout the ancestral narratives.[47] Jacob had four wives; Jacob's brother Esau had five;[48] Gideon had many (together they produced seventy sons for him[49]); and Elkanah, the father of the prophet Samuel, had two.[50] Polygyny continued to be practiced well into the biblical period, and it is attested among Jews as late as the second century CE.[51] In the original version of the book of Esther, its heroine's inclusion in the Persian king's harem is presented matter-of-factly.

Opponents of same-sex marriage often assert that from the beginning marriage has been between one man and one woman. Well, yes and no: in the beginning, according to Genesis, there was only the original couple in the Garden of Eden, no one else with whom either could have any sort of relationship;[52] but Genesis never reports a marriage ceremony. Not long after Eden, however, the biblical writers tell us, men began to have more than one wife, beginning with Cain's descendant Lamech, who had two wives, Adah and Zillah.[53] So, with the authority of the Bible behind them, early Mormons argued for "plural marriage," and some Mormon fundamentalist sects continue to practice polygyny. They were and are right: if the Bible provides authoritative models, then a man should be allowed to have more than one wife, as did Abraham, Jacob, David, and other biblical heroes, with no hint of divine disapproval.

Polygyny had a payoff: it increased the number of offspring, who were valuable in their own right as sources of labor. It also was a status symbol, showing that a man or his family had the assets to come up with brideprices for and to support several wives. Moreover, polygyny is presumed in biblical law. Here is an example:

> If a man has two wives, one loved and the other hated, and if both the loved one and the hated one have borne him sons, the firstborn being the son of the hated one, then on the day when he gives his sons their inheritance of his property, he should not make the son of the loved one the firstborn instead of the son of the hated one, who is the firstborn. He must recognize as firstborn the son of the hated one, giving him a double portion of all that he has; since he is the first of his power, the right of the firstborn is his.[54]

In the context of the Bible as a whole, it is hard not to see this as an indirect critique of how Abraham treated Hagar. But it is not a critique of polygyny as such.

What the law does suggest is that wives of the same

husband had a different status. Anthropologists call these "primary" and "secondary" wives. One of the terms biblical writers use for the latter is often translated as "concubine," but in the Bible it does not have its usual meaning in English, of a mistress; it denotes a secondary wife, either a free woman or a slave.

There are several dozen references to such secondary wives in biblical texts from all periods, showing that the practice was widespread. One recurring example is the royal harem, which consisted of both primary and secondary wives. Such harems are reported for several of the kings of Israel, from the beginning to the end of the monarchy. David had eight or more wives, in addition to "concubines,"[55] and Solomon reportedly had seven hundred wives and three hundred concubines,[56] making him the greatest lover of all (which might explain why he is credited with writing the Song of Solomon). Solomon's multiple marriages are condemned, not because of their number but because many of his wives were non-Israelites and caused him to worship their gods.[57]

Many marriages of the kings of Israel and Judah are best described as politically motivated. As has been true of rulers from antiquity to the modern era, marriage between a king and the daughter of a neighboring monarch or tribal leader, or between their children, strengthened the ties between the kings and their realms. In the Bible, David, Solomon, Ahab, and several of the Herods are among those of whom such marriages are reported;

realpolitik trumped the principle of endogamy. Having a harem also demonstrated a king's power, prestige, and wealth.

In royal families, sex and politics were connected in another way. A successor or usurper to the throne of a ruling monarch showed his own power and correspondingly his predecessor's lack of it by taking possession of the predecessor's harem. After Saul's death, Abner, his general, slept with one of Saul's wives, perhaps in a move to gain power for himself.[58] Other wives of Saul became part of the harem of David, his successor.[59] Then, during the short-lived revolt of David's son Absalom against his father, he publicly took possession of—"went into"—his father's harem, demonstrating that he had replaced David as ruler.[60]

Another example of how sex and power were connected occurs at the end of David's life. The old king apparently had bad circulation, for "although they covered him with garments, he could not get warm." So his officials held the first beauty contest in recorded history. Searching throughout all Israel, they found a virgin, Abishag the Shunammite, to lie with him. And so she did—she became the king's attendant, but "the king did not know her."[61] So David was not just moribund, but also impotent, and not just sexually, but also politically, and the court intrigue concerning succession immediately began. That resulted in Solomon, David's son by Bathsheba, becoming king, even though important factions in the court backed his older brother Adonijah (whose mother was Haggith). After David died, Adonijah asked Bathsheba to ask Solomon to give him Abishag, David's last sleeping companion. Solomon knew that this was a challenge to his rule, even if Bathsheba did not, and he immediately ordered that Adonijah, his half brother, be executed.[62]

We find expropriation of royal harems as a demonstration of power in other contexts too. When the Assyrian king Sennacherib invaded Judah at the end of the eighth century BCE, and forced its ruler, Hezekiah, to surrender, part of the extensive tribute Hezekiah paid were his own daughters and his palace women.[63] The delivery of the defeated king's harem to his conqueror showed the victor's power.

This treatment of women in royal harems is a stark example of how women in the ancient Near East could be depersonalized. The same transfer of wives is also attributed to God; speaking in the name of the LORD, the prophet Jeremiah proclaims that as punishment for the Israelites' disobedience to divine commands,

> I will give their wives to others,
> and their fields to dispossessors.[64]

Even for the deity, women were property to be transferred as circumstances warranted.

The New Testament adds little to this picture. We find

one actual wedding, that at Cana,[65] and many references to marriage in parable and metaphor, but no indication of how these marriages were contracted. Nonbiblical evidence suggests that arranged marriages continued to be the norm. And the status of the wife is the same—she is "saved through childbearing,"[66] and is to be subordinate to her husband, in a divinely established gender imbalance:

> Wives should be subordinate to their husbands.... For the husband is the head of the wife, just as Christ is the head of the church....Just as the church is subordinate to Christ, so wives should be to their husbands in everything. Husbands, love your wives, as Christ loved the church.[67]

The Western idea of romantic love is not entirely absent in the Bible, however. As in English, the Hebrew word for "love" can have a wide spectrum of meaning—from amorous desire to the most profound selfless affection, from the erotic to the exalted. "Love" can mean infatuation, even sexual obsession, as when we are told that Amnon loved Tamar before he raped her.[68] Jacob also loved Rachel, who was "beautiful in form and in appearance," long before they were married.[69] In the only explicit narrative mention of a woman loving a man, Michal loved David, apparently from a distance.[70] In these cases, "love" must mean physical attraction. And Solomon loved many foreign women—that is, they became part of his extensive harem, available for his pleasure.[71]

Nor do I mean to suggest that arranged marriages are intrinsically inferior to the modern Western model of falling in love. In both ancient and present-day societies where arranged marriages have been the norm, profound love has often been as much a part of those relationships as it has been in the West with its insistence on the romantic ideal. According to biblical writers, a loving marriage was enjoyed by couples such as Isaac and Rebekah;[72] Samuel's parents, Elkanah and Hannah;[73] and the prophet Ezekiel and his wife—"the delight of his eyes."[74]

DIVORCE

When Sarah, Abraham's primary wife, saw Ishmael, the son of Hagar, Abraham's secondary wife, "making her son laugh," she told Abraham to "expel this slave woman and her son." Abraham sadly agreed, after God told him to do what Sarah had said—and "he sent her away."[75] The two words used here—"expel" and "send away"—are those used for divorce in other passages, so by implication Abraham divorced Hagar, and with divine approval. Both verbs powerfully express the legal and psychological violence of the rupture.

Judging from its occasional mention in the Bible as well as in nonbiblical sources, divorce was practiced in biblical times, although it was frowned upon. The evidence, however, is incomplete and inconsistent, in widely scattered texts from different periods. One reason for this less-than-full treatment may be that, as in other societies where marriages are arranged, divorce was infrequent.

The process of divorce is detailed in one law:

> If a man takes a wife and marries her, and then if she does not find favor in his eyes because he found in her nakedness of a thing, and he then writes for her a certificate of divorce, and puts it in her hand and sends her from his house, and when she has left his house, and she goes to become another man's wife, if the second husband hates her and writes a certificate of divorce and puts it in her hand and sends her from his house, or if the second husband who took her as a wife dies, then her first husband who sent her out is not permitted to return to take her so that she becomes his wife after she has become impure; that would be an abomination before Yahweh, and you should not make the land that Yahweh your God gave you sinful.[76]

The law itself, one very long sentence in the original Hebrew, is not primarily about divorce, but about a man not remarrying a wife he had divorced, after she had married again and then been divorced or widowed by her second husband. No reason is given for this prohibition; it may have had to do with issues of paternity and inheritance, as well as perhaps with a sense that reestablishing a sexual relationship with a woman who had been with another man violated some taboo.[77] But the law does describe how divorce took place in ancient Israel: a man gave his wife a legally binding certificate of divorce—literally, "a document of cutting off"[78]— and sent her away.

This law also gives one reason for divorce: the wife did not find favor in her husband's eyes because of "nakedness of a thing," a phrase that occurs only one other time in the Bible, where it refers to indecent exposure during defecation.[79] In this case, although "nakedness" refers to the genitals, something short of adultery may be meant—like Isaac making Rebekah "laugh," perhaps—because adultery was a capital crime.[80] On the other hand, a husband whose wife had been unfaithful could choose another course, as Joseph planned to do when he discovered Mary's pregnancy: "Because he was righteous and did not wish to make her offense public, he wanted to divorce her secretly."[81]

Why, other than "nakedness of a thing," would a man divorce his wife? One law suggests that simple dissatisfaction was a legitimate basis.[82] Another was conflict between wives of the same man, as with Sarah and Hagar. And there may have been other reasons, judging from the mention of divorced women in other contexts—for example, a priest's daughter, if she had been divorced and had returned to her father's house, was allowed to share in the priestly portions of sacrifices offered by worshippers.[83]

In the Hebrew Bible, divorce is prohibited in two specific cases. In one, a man who wants to divorce his wife claims that when they were married she was not a virgin. Her parents can refute this charge by bringing—improbably—the bloody sheet from the wedding night, apparently given to the father to keep just for this eventuality. If the charge turns out to be true, or at least no contrary evidence is provided, then the woman is to be executed by stoning at the entrance to her father's house, "because she did folly in Israel by being promiscuous in her father's house."[84] But if the evidence is provided, the husband is fined one hundred shekels, "because he has damaged the reputation of a virgin in Israel."[85] The fine is given to the girl's father—it is ultimately his honor that has been besmirched, because he has been falsely accused of not acting as a father should, keeping his daughter intact.[86] Moreover, the husband is prohibited from ever divorcing the woman. This may have assuaged the woman's father's honor (as did the fine), and even provided some security for the woman—but it seems unfair to require a woman to continue living with a man who "hates" her.[87] The same prohibition, for the same reasons, applies to a man who rapes a virgin, according to Deuteronomy's variant of an earlier law in Exodus: he must marry her, and he cannot ever divorce her.[88]

Priests were prohibited from marrying divorced women, as well as promiscuous women and women who had been "pierced" (presumably raped), and the high priest in particular was also banned from marrying a widow. He, of whom the highest level of ritual purity was required, could marry only "a virgin of his own people."[89] Like a widow and a rape victim, a divorced woman was used goods, beneath the holiness required of the priesthood.

So, on the few occasions that the Hebrew Bible mentions divorce, it is permissible, although sometimes with a stigma attached. This is the case with an extremely difficult passage in the book of Malachi:

> You cover Yahweh's altar with tears,
>> with weeping and groaning,
> because he no longer regards the offering
>> nor accepts favor from your hand.
> You say, "Why?"
> Because Yahweh was a witness between you and the
>> wife of your youth,
>> with whom you acted treacherously,
> even though she is your companion,
>> and your wife by covenant.
> . . . . .
> So do not act treacherously with the wife of your youth.
> If a man hates [his wife] and sends her away
>> [divorces her], says Yahweh, the god of Israel,
> then he covers his garment with violence, says
> Yahweh of hosts.[90]

The usual translation of the beginning of the last verse is "'I hate divorce,' says the LORD," but such an absolute statement misrepresents the admittedly opaque

Hebrew. Furthermore, it is inconsistent with earlier biblical law, supposedly divinely given, as well as with Yahweh's own divorce of Israel—according to the prophet Jeremiah, speaking in the name of the LORD, and using the metaphor of God as Israel's husband, God proclaims: "Because of the repeated adultery of rebellious Israel, I sent her away and I gave her a certificate of divorce."[91] To be sure, such inconsistency is not surprising, given the nature of the Bible as an anthology of writings by many different people at many different times.

The book of Malachi dates to the fifth century BCE, when one of the main issues in Judah was exogamy, marriage outside the group. The passage may refer to Jewish men divorcing their Jewish wives in order to marry non-Jewish women, implicitly younger women—trophy wives, perhaps. Such intermarriage was unequivocally opposed by the leaders Ezra and Nehemiah, with whom the book of Malachi may be contemporary. In the book of Ezra, a spokesman for the community in Jerusalem admits their collective guilt.

> We have been unfaithful to our God, and have brought home foreign women from the peoples of the land. Yet there is hope for Israel despite this. Let us now make a covenant with our God to expel all these women and those born to them.[92]

According to one ancient tradition,[93] they then forced the foreign women to leave, with their children, just as

Abraham had done to his wife Hagar and their son, Ishmael. Remarkably, even horribly, endogamy was more important than paternal custody or family stability. Malachi may be part of this discussion, criticizing the practice of divorcing one's Jewish wife in order to marry a foreign woman. If this guess is right, then in its context the passage in Malachi is more about exogamy than about divorce as such. And even if the usual translation is correct, this text need not be privileged over others.

The incomplete and inconsistent picture of divorce in the Hebrew Bible meant that as its texts came to be considered authoritative, debate continued on how they were to be interpreted. We find evidence of such debate in the New Testament, but the views of its writers were no more consistent than those of the Jewish scriptures.

The first three Gospels of the New Testament are called the Synoptic Gospels, because when looked at together they are remarkably similar. This is because they are related, in a literary way. In antiquity, liberal borrowing from another author's work was commonplace. Modern notions of copyright did not exist, and such borrowing, found often in the Bible, was not considered plagiarism. According to a majority of scholars, Mark was the earliest Gospel (although written several decades after Jesus's death), and it was used as a source by both Matthew and Luke. They often copied what Mark had written—sometimes correcting Mark's mistakes, sometimes rearranging his presentation, sometimes expanding and deleting, but often following him closely. Matthew and Luke must also have shared another source, because there are a large number of sayings of Jesus that are the same in those two Gospels but are not found in Mark.[94] Both writers used these sources freely, reflecting their own cultural backgrounds. The result is that we cannot know exactly what Jesus said about anything, let alone what he may have thought: every word of Jesus is refracted through the lenses of the Gospel writers.

Here are some of Jesus's reported sayings about divorce:

- Whoever divorces his wife and marries another woman has committed adultery against her. And if she divorces her husband and marries another man, she commits adultery.[95]
- Whoever divorces his wife except for indecency and marries another woman commits adultery.[96]
- Every man who divorces his wife and marries another woman commits adultery, and whoever marries a woman divorced from her husband commits adultery.[97]

Underlying these different formulations is what was plausibly Jesus's own view: he opposed remarriage after a divorce, and thus at least implicitly divorce as well, although no reason is given for his opposition in these related sayings.

The differences among the various formulations are revealing. In the first version, from Mark's Gospel, divorce could apparently be initiated by a wife as well as a husband. In the second version, from Matthew (as also in Luke, the third version), there is no recognition that a wife could initiate divorce, and it is closer to what Jesus probably said, because in his milieu, subject to biblical law, only the husband could initiate a divorce. But Mark, many scholars think, was written for an audience of Gentile believers in Jesus, and in that milieu, subject to Roman law, women did have the right to sue for divorce, so Mark expands the saying of Jesus to apply to his context.

The second version, from Matthew, allows for an exception to the prohibition of divorce that the other two do not. Matthew and his audience were, scholars think, Jewish Christians—Jewish believers in Jesus who remained Jewish in matters of belief and observance but also accepted Jesus as Messiah. The exception Jesus allows according to Matthew is, not surprisingly, taken from biblical law: "except for indecency" is a free translation, an interpretation really, of "nakedness of a thing" in the law in Deuteronomy. If Jesus himself followed biblical law, then he would have allowed divorce for the reason found in Deuteronomy, as Matthew reports.

In Mark's Gospel, the first saying of Jesus quoted above is given, as often in Mark, only to his disciples, in private, after a public exchange between Jesus and the Pharisees. Such encounters occur frequently in the

Gospels; they are a literary device meant to show that
Jesus is wiser than those guardians of Torah observance.
In this confrontation,

> Pharisees came and questioned him whether it
> was permissible for a man to send away his wife—
> they were testing him. In reply he said to them,
> "What did Moses command you?" They said,
> "Moses allowed a man to write a certificate of
> divorce and send [his wife] away." Jesus said to
> them, "Because of the hardness of your hearts he
> wrote this command. But from the beginning of
> creation 'male and female he made them.' 'For
> this reason a man leaves his father and mother
> and attaches himself to his wife, and the two
> become one flesh.' So they are no longer two
> but one flesh. Therefore what God has joined
> together, let no one separate."[98]

We are listening in on an inner-Jewish debate about
divorce. Both sides quote scripture as their authority—
the Torah, written, it was believed, by Moses himself.
The Pharisees are right: Deuteronomy does allow
divorce. But Jesus refutes their argument with the aston-
ishing assertion that this law is not authoritative. Rather,
it was a concession to the Israelites' stubbornness,
implicitly like that of the Pharaoh who oppressed them
before the Exodus from Egypt.[99] In support of his argument Jesus cites Genesis 1.27 and 2.24.

The problem with Rabbi Jesus's argument, I would

say, were I a Pharisee, is that the first text he quotes is about gender differentiation, not marriage or divorce: God created humans (and presumably all other animals, too, although the text does not say so) male and female. The second text Jesus quotes, from the narrative of the Garden of Eden, is about the origin of the heterosexual drive: a once-androgynous creature, separated into man and woman by the LORD, has a powerful urge to restore its original unity—"one flesh." Finally, neither text explicitly mentions marriage, let alone divorce. Were Adam and Eve married? Again, Genesis does not say. And if they were to divorce, who else could they marry?

For Mark, Jesus bests the Pharisees. Divorce, he says, is not part of the original divine intent, and scripture proves it. So Jesus was opposed to divorce, at least in principle. Yet his reasoning is flawed: like believers throughout the ages, he bases his argument on scripture, but the passages he reportedly quotes are not really apropos. Jesus is also selective in his appeal to scriptural authority, cavalierly dismissing a law given by Moses in Deuteronomy because it is inconsistent with his own view.

There is another version in Matthew's Gospel of the sayings we first looked at:

> It was said, "Whoever divorces his wife, let him give her a certificate of divorce." But I say to you that every man who divorces his wife, except in the matter of indecency, makes her commit adultery. And whoever marries a divorced woman commits adultery.[100]

Found in the Sermon on the Mount, this saying, like Matthew's shorter version of the same saying, allows for divorce "in the matter of indecency," a more literal translation of "nakedness of a thing." And, as in the debate with the Pharisees, it shows Jesus again rejecting scriptural authority.

Jesus's opposition to divorce is also mentioned in one of the earliest writings of the New Testament, Paul's first letter to the Corinthians:

> To those who are married I command—rather not I, but the Lord—that a wife should not separate from her husband—but if she does separate, she should remain unmarried or be reconciled to her husband—and a man should not send his wife away.[101]

Paul knows the teaching of Jesus, and cites it as authoritative—"not I, but the Lord." According to Paul, more clearly than in the Gospels, Jesus was opposed not just to remarriage after divorce but to divorce itself—a reasonable and not entirely surprising view, both because of the stigma attached to divorce in earlier biblical tradition and because of the disruptive nature of divorce itself. Yet Paul, even though aware of Jesus's view, allows for divorce: "...if she does separate...." Also, despite his own deep background in Judaism, when writing to Gentile Christians at Corinth in Greece, who were subject to Roman jurisdiction,

Paul, like Mark, recognized that divorce could be initiated by either party.

Moreover, despite his opposition to divorce in principle, Paul allows for divorce for a reason other than that given in Deuteronomy and by Jesus in the Gospel of Matthew:

> To the rest, I say—not the Lord: if any brother has an unbelieving wife, and she is willing to live with him, he should not divorce her. And if any woman has an unbelieving husband and he is willing to live with her, she should not divorce her husband. For the unbelieving man is made holy through the wife, and the unbelieving wife is made holy through the brother. Otherwise your children would be unclean; but now they are holy. But if the unbelieving man wishes to be divorced, let him be divorced. In such cases neither the brother nor the sister is bound. God has called you to peace.[102]

Paul here is addressing a situation that must have been frequent in the early decades of Christianity: one partner in a marriage became a Christian, and the other, troubled or even disgusted by his or her spouse's involvement with this fringe cult, wanted out. In that case, Paul says, divorce is allowed. So, despite Jesus's general condemnation of divorce, for Paul in some circumstances it is better than the alternative—lack of domestic tranquillity. Just as Jesus apparently felt free to reject the authority of Moses, so Paul, who thought that he knew what Jesus said, on his own authority—"I say, not the Lord"—also felt free to modify Jesus's teaching in the light of changed circumstances.

In general, then, biblical writers did not think that divorce was a good thing. But for many of them, divorce was allowable, probably because they thought it better than an unhappy marriage. I think it significant that no New Testament writer quotes Malachi's obscure pronouncement—perhaps the text was as opaque to them as it is to me.

Given the Bible's unsystematic treatment of divorce, it is not surprising that communities of faith that accept the Bible's authority differ greatly among themselves on the issue. In Judaism, divorce is allowed, although traditionally, following Deuteronomy, only the husband can initiate it. Protestants and Eastern Orthodox Christians, extrapolating from the exceptions allowed in Matthew and in Paul, generally allow divorce, although with variations from church to church.

Roman Catholicism prohibits divorce under most circumstances. The *Catechism of the Catholic Church*[103] cites Jesus's words in Mark, which do not provide any exception, as its scriptural authority—a blatantly selective use of scripture, ignoring Matthew's different view. The increasingly widespread practice of annulment, however, undercuts this prohibition: some fifty thousand Catholics receive annulments from their local bishops each year in the United States. Despite the casuistic distinction between divorce and annulment made by church authorities, such annulments are the functional equivalent of divorce, allowing the spouse to remarry with ecclesiastical approval.

There are two situations, however, in which divorce is permissible for Roman Catholics. One, called the Petrine privilege because it can only be given by the pope, allows a Catholic to divorce from an unbaptized partner if he or she wishes to marry someone who is baptized: the principle of endogamy is more important than the supposed indissolubility of marriage. The other, called the Pauline privilege, is based on words of Paul in 1 Corinthians: if one partner in a marriage converts to Catholicism and the non-Catholic partner takes offense, a divorce may take place. So much for "from the beginning it was not so"[104]— Jesus's insistence that divorce is contrary to the Creator's intent.

For both marriage and divorce, then, scripture is an inadequate guide: pervasively patriarchal, as well as inconsistent. Yet scripture also empowers individuals and communities who accept it as authoritative to move beyond it. Jesus rejects the teaching of Moses and the Torah, Paul goes beyond the teaching of Jesus, and likewise believers through the ages and especially in modern times have selectively adopted, adapted, and even rejected what the Bible says about marriage and divorce.

CHAPTER 4

THOU SHALT NOT

Forbidden Sexual Relationships
in the Bible

Bathsheba Bathing, from the Hours of Marguerite de Coetivy, ca. 1490–1500. The scenes in the margins are subsequent episodes in the narrative.

"Enjoy life with the woman you love," advises the author of Ecclesiastes.[1] Here and there the Bible celebrates human love and marital sex, especially for its reproductive results. But the Bible is more famous, even infamous, for its prohibitions and condemnations of what in its writers' views was sex with the wrong people or at the wrong time.

ADULTERY

The Decalogue, the Ten Commandments, is the most important legal code in the Bible, and it has continued to be so for Jews and especially for Christians. Yet although the Decalogue is often understood as a set of universal laws, in its original context in the book of Exodus its audience is narrow: the Israelites whom God had just freed from Egyptian bondage, now standing at Sinai.[2] And not even all the Israelites. Modern translations obscure the identification of those to whom the Decalogue is addressed. In Hebrew, all ten commands are in the second person masculine singular—that is, they are addressed only to Israelite males.

Just one of the Ten Commandments deals specifically with sex: the seventh, "Thou shalt not commit adultery."[3] It forbids Israelite men to have sexual relationships with other Israelites' wives. Because marriage was a contractual transaction in which a woman, as property, was transferred from her father to her husband, in exchange for a bride-price, adultery was in effect expropriation of property. Moreover, because it could raise questions about paternity, adultery complicated inheritance in the patriarchal social structure, in which a man's estate was passed on to his sons when he died.[4]

The status of the wife as property is made clear in the last commandment.

> You shall not covet your neighbor's house; you shall not covet your neighbor's wife, or male or female slave, or ox, or donkey, or anything that belongs to your neighbor.[5]

In general, this commandment puts off-limits the neighbor's property, listed in descending order of value: the wife is worth less than the real estate but more than slaves and livestock.

Although often interpreted as simply "desiring," the Hebrew word traditionally translated "covet" is ambiguous. It can mean "to desire" or "to crave," but it also has the nuance of "plot to get control of." The prophet Micah describes evildoers as

> those who think of wickedness
> and evil deeds on their beds.
> In the light of morning they do it,
> because it is in the grasp of their hands.
> They covet fields and seize them,
> houses and take them.[6]

The thought is father to the action, and both are wrong. Coveting, then, was not just psychological, but also practical: it was the first step in the illicit seizure of property, and that is what it means in the last commandment: you shall not conspire to expropriate your neighbor's property, including his wife by committing adultery with her.[7] The commandment's prohibition is thus a narrow one. Because it is addressed to men, it does not explicitly prohibit women from having sex with married men, or, for that matter, prohibit married men from having sex with unmarried women, including prostitutes. Still, preachers and moralists have tended to interpret the commandment as a comprehensive ban of what they consider sexual immorality. The *Catechism of the Catholic Church* provides an example of this tendency, including in its discussion of this commandment prostitution, pornography, rape, artificial birth control, incest, masturbation, premarital sex, divorce, polygamy, and homosexuality.[8] But Jesus apparently held a less expansive interpretation. In the Sermon on the Mount, as part of a series of contrasts between the Torah and his preaching, he says in Matthew's Gospel:

> You have heard that it was said, "You shall not commit adultery." But I say to you that everyone who looks at a woman with desire has already committed adultery with her in his heart.[9]

Like the commandments in the Decalogue, this saying of Jesus is addressed to men.[10] And in the interpretation of Rabbi Jesus, the commandment has to do with adultery as such, not with lust or desire, although he disapproves of that, too.

The penalty for adultery was death.

> If a man commits adultery with his neighbor's wife, both the adulterer and the adulteress shall be put to death.[11]

> If a man is found sleeping with another man's wife, both of them—the man who slept with the woman and the woman—shall die.[12]

David and Bathsheba

The understanding of adultery as expropriation of another man's property is also found in biblical narrative.

The most famous adulterer in the Bible—in fact, the only named male adulterer—is David, Israel's second king. In the vivid account of the latter part of David's reign in 2 Samuel, we are introduced to a dark side of this complex character, up to this point depicted in heroic terms. One episode in a shocking series of revelations about him begins:

> In the spring, the time when kings go forth to war, David sent Joab and his servants and all Israel to ravage the Ammonites and to lay siege to Rabbah; but David stayed in Jerusalem.[13]

David had been a mighty warrior, as legends and earlier historical notes about him in the Bible elaborate. Now, in an offensive after the winter rains during which movement of troops and chariots would have been difficult, David's army was attacking the Ammonite capital of Rabbah (modern Amman), in Transjordan. But David was not with them. The narrator slyly implies that had David been leading his army in the field as a king should, what follows would not have taken place.

Ancient Near Eastern cities were crowded, because everyone had to be within the walls in case of attack. Jerusalem was no exception, except that it was barely a city—by our standards, just a village. In David's time, its population was only a few thousand, who lived on about a dozen acres, roughly equal to two blocks in Midtown Manhattan. Early in his reign, David had captured this fortified town, made it his capital, and built in it a palace for himself. This royal residence probably was higher than nearby houses, to elevate the king above the smoke and smells and sounds of the dense town. Like the houses surrounding it, and like many houses in the Middle East then and now, it had a flat roof.

One evening, while walking on his roof after his afternoon nap, David caught sight of a beautiful woman bathing—literally, "washing herself"—in a nearby house, either on the roof or in the enclosed courtyard. Was this just a coincidence? Did David like to look down from his high roof on the city he ruled? Was he a voyeur, a Peeping Tom? Did he know that the woman next door liked to bathe at this time of day? Or did Bathsheba know of the king's habits, and was her self-exposure calculated? The parsimonious narrator leaves such questions unanswered.

When David asked about the woman he had seen, he learned that she was Bathsheba, wife of one of his elite warriors, Uriah the Hittite. Even so, he sent for her and slept with her. The narrator tells us in an aside that her washing was the purification bath after menstruation; Bathsheba therefore was not pregnant. But she was in the fertile period of her menstrual cycle, and David's intercourse with her resulted in pregnancy. She informs David of her condition in the only words she speaks in this episode: "I am pregnant."[14] David immediately takes action, summoning Uriah from the battlefield "to wash his feet"—that is, as Uriah himself recognized, to sleep with his wife—so that he would be thought the father of the child. But even though David got him drunk, Uriah refused: as a participant in holy war, he was supposed to refrain from sex.[15] So David sent him back to the battlefield with a sealed note to his general Joab that in effect was Uriah's death warrant: "Put Uriah in the fiercest part of the battle, and then retreat from him so that he may be hit and die."[16] The order was carried out, and David became not just an adulterer but a murderer by proxy, who, coveting his neighbor's wife, had plotted to make her his own.

In response, Yahweh sent the prophet Nathan to David, who presented him with a case of the sort that kings were supposed to adjudicate.

> There were two men in the same city, one rich and one poor. The rich man had sheep and cattle in abundance, but the poor man had only a small lamb which he had bought and raised with his sons. It used to eat his scraps and drink from his cup and lie in his arms, so that it was like a daughter to him. One day a visitor came to the rich man. But he was unwilling to take one of his sheep or his cattle to prepare for the traveler who had come to him. Rather, he took the poor man's lamb and prepared it for the man who had come to him.[17]

David replied with outrage, ordering that the man pay compensatory and punitive damages. But then Nathan proclaimed, "You are the man!"[18]

Recognizing his guilt, David asked for divine forgiveness, which was granted to him, although the child to be born had to die as vicarious punishment. The guilt of the father was transferred to his son—hardly a fair principle, but consistent with the Decalogue's view of intergenerational guilt: God himself punishes sons for the sin of their fathers.[19] Subsequently David married Bathsheba, his eighth wife, and their second son, Solomon, eventually succeeded David on the throne.

As the fictional case concocted by Nathan shows, just as the rich man took the poor man's lamb, so, in committing adultery with Bathsheba, David was guilty of expropriating Uriah's property, his wife Bathsheba.[20]

SEX WITH FAMILY MEMBERS

Adultery is also prohibited in the book of Leviticus:

> You shall not have sex with your kinsman's wife, to defile yourself with her.[21]

This prohibition occurs in the context of a list of about twenty forbidden sexual relationships. A man is prohibited from having sex with his mother, another of his father's wives, his sister, his daughter-in-law, his aunt, and his sister-in-law.[22] In each case, the reason is the same, as a literal translation of the last prohibition shows: "You shall not uncover your brother's wife's nakedness: it is your brother's nakedness."[23] "Nakedness" is a circumlocution for what the Romans called "pudenda" ("shameful things")—in our euphemism, "private parts," the genitals. The "nakedness" of a man's sister-in-law belongs to her husband, his brother; uncovering it—in sex—is a violation of his rights. The same formula is used for most of the other prohibitions. In other words, women who belonged to a male relative were off-limits. A variant of the first prohibition reinforces this interpretation:

> Cursed be anyone who sleeps with his father's wife, because he has uncovered his father's skirt.[24]

A man who sleeps with his father's wife—not his mother, presumably, although this is not stated—has usurped his father's right to that woman, who is, again, the father's property.

Not all of these prohibitions concern what we would call incest, sex between close relatives. As with the seventh commandment, they have to do with property: one man in an extended family expropriating the property of another man in the same family, a woman under the latter's control. That is why the list is incomplete according to our definition of incest: sex between a father and his daughter is not mentioned, because the daughter was the father's property, as the law permitting a man to sell his daughter as a slave shows.[25] If a man had sex with his daughter, there was no one he could prosecute for her loss of value.[26]

Did the prohibition against having sex with women who belonged to another man in one's extended family also rule out marriage to such women? Leviticus is not explicit on this point, although in some narratives marrying one's half sister was possible.

Tamar

Genesis relates the story of a woman named Tamar, who had been married to Er, the oldest son of the patriarch Judah, one of Jacob's twelve sons. But Er had died suddenly: the text says that he was wicked, and Yahweh put him to death. According to a law in Deuteronomy, when a man died without a son, it was his brother's obligation to marry his widow. The first son she bore would continue the dead brother's line, carry his name, and inherit his property; legally he would be considered the son of his father's dead brother rather than of his biological father.[27]

In accordance with this requirement, Judah ordered his second son, Onan, to carry out his duty as a brother-in-law: "to raise up seed for your brother."[28] Knowing that the "seed" would not be his, whenever Onan went into his dead brother's wife, he spilled his seed on the ground. Although Onan gives his name to "onanism," usually a synonym for masturbation, Onan was not masturbating but practicing coitus interruptus. This displeased Yahweh, so he put Onan to death as well.

Unaware of why his sons had died, Judah concluded that Tamar was the problem. Folklore often tells of such "dangerous brides," as in the book of Tobit, where each of the seven successive husbands of a woman named Sarah had died in the bridal chamber on the night of the wedding—allegedly because of a demon.[29] So Judah sent Tamar back to her father's house, telling her that she could marry his third son, Shelah, when he was old enough. But Judah had no such intention.

Eventually, to avoid being childless, Tamar took matters into her own hands, disguising herself as a prostitute on the road that she knew Judah would be traveling on his way to the annual spring sheepshearing. He fell for the bait and, promising payment later, gave her his seal and his staff as security pledge. Then he "went into her," and she became pregnant. After the transaction she removed her disguise, and went home. Three months later, Tamar's pregnancy was reported to Judah, who ordered her burned to death[30] for promiscuity;[31] as the widow of his sons, she was under his control, even though living in her father's house. Tamar, however, produced the seal and staff, which Judah recognized as his, and he pardoned her. In due course she gave birth to twin boys, one of whom, Perez, was King David's ancestor.[32]

Both the law in Deuteronomy and the story of Tamar that illustrates it are inconsistent with the prohibition in Leviticus of sleeping with a brother's wife.[33] Perhaps that applied only if the brother was alive, or perhaps

Leviticus, compiled later than Deuteronomy, is a repudiation of the earlier requirement of preserving an older brother's name by fathering children with his widow. In any case, Judah's intercourse with Tamar is not explicitly criticized, even though she was his daughter-in-law and technically belonged to his youngest surviving son. And Tamar is praised for having forced him to do what was right, although the narrator reports that Judah "did not know her again."[34]

Sex between close relatives also appears in the story of another woman named Tamar, one of David's daughters, who was raped by her half brother Amnon.[35] As in the case of the first Tamar, details in the narrative about her are inconsistent with the laws we have been considering. Leviticus directly addresses the situation:

> You shall not uncover the nakedness of your sister, the daughter of your father or the daughter of your mother.[36]

There are two related issues: could a man have sex with his half sister, to whom he was not married? Certainly not, especially if it was rape, which is unequivocally condemned. But could a man marry his half sister? Before the rape, Tamar pleaded with Amnon to ask their father, David, to give her to Amnon as a wife. So Tamar seemed to think that marriage between half siblings was possible. Abraham apparently did too: in one passage in Genesis he claims that Sarah is both his wife and his half sister.[37] Even though this claim may be suspect, the narrator of this particular version of the wife-sister tale[38] did not consider it out of the question for a man and his half sister to be married. In our culture such a marriage would be incestuous.

Lot's Daughters

There is another case of what we call incest in biblical narrative. The only survivors of God's destruction of Sodom (for reasons to which we will soon turn) were Lot and his two unmarried daughters. The women thought that no one else on earth was alive, so to ensure that they would have children, on successive nights they got their father drunk and slept with him. From these unions were born, we are told, the ancestors of Israel's neighbors to the east, the Ammonites and the Moabites.[39] This is one of several narratives about the legendary ancestors of non-Israelite groups in Genesis that attribute to them sexual practices the Israelites considered reprehensible. It recalls an earlier, and similarly motivated, narrative, in which one of Noah's sons, Ham, looked at his drunken father's nakedness; for this offense, Ham's son Canaan was cursed.[40] On its face, this brief tale about Noah has to do with exposure of his genitals, but it has overtones of homosexual and incestuous rape. As with Lot, drunkenness is followed by sex with family members, and those cases of incest were considered taboo by the narrators.

Reuben

Violation of the prohibition of sex with a woman under another man's control briefly figures in the history of Reuben, the oldest of Jacob's children. In a brief note we are told, "Reuben went and lay with Bilhah, his father's concubine, and Israel [Jacob] heard of it."[41] As with some other prose narratives in the Bible, there is an older poetic account of this episode, in Jacob's death-bed blessing of his sons.

> Reuben, you are my firstborn:
> > my might, and the first of my power,
> > excelling in rank, and excelling in strength....
> But you will excel no longer,
> > for you climbed into your father's bed,
> you defiled my couch.[42]

Reuben, the son of Leah, Jacob's first wife, had sex with Bilhah, the servant of Rachel, Leah's sister and Jacob's second wife, with whom Jacob had fathered Gad and Naphtali: Bilhah was thus a secondary wife of Jacob, like Leah's servant Zilpah. In other words, Reuben was guilty of violating the prohibition against intercourse with one's father's wife, and he was punished by being demoted from his status of firstborn son and principal heir.

This legend is what scholars call an etiology, an explanation of the origin of a custom, social reality, geographical feature, or the like: in this case, it explains why the tribe of Reuben, once so powerful, had diminished in importance. It is also another illustration of the tendency to attribute unacceptable sexual behavior to outsiders, for Reuben's territory was east of the Jordan River and thus beyond the conventional borders of the Promised Land. Reuben's action may have had political overtones as well, as with David's son Absalom, when he "went into" his father's concubines, and Adonijah, when he asked that King Solomon give him David's last concubine as his wife.

OTHER PROHIBITED SEXUAL RELATIONSHIPS

Following the list of prohibited relationships between a man and women under another man's control, Leviticus 18 continues with other prohibitions. The first forbids having sex with a woman during her period:

> You shall not approach a woman to uncover her nakedness during her menstrual impurity.[43]

The primal taboo about reproductive emissions of both men and women is found frequently in the Bible. Ejaculation makes a man ritually impure for a day—for this reason, men were prohibited from having sex while engaged in holy war.[44] If ejaculation occurs during sex with a woman, she too is impure for the rest of the day.[45] In females, other normal vaginal emissions, including not just menstruation but discharges associated with childbirth, also make them impure.[46]

Two further prohibitions follow:

> You shall not lie with a male as with a woman: that is an abomination. You shall not have sex with any animal, to defile yourself; and a woman should not present herself to an animal to crossbreed with it: that is perversion.[47]

The same prohibitions are found in Leviticus 20, where the penalty for both offenses is death for all parties, including the animals in the case of bestiality.[48]

The juxtaposition of bestiality and male homoerotic relationships is revealing. Bestiality is prohibited because it entails a mixing of natural categories as the ancients understood them. Similarly, if a man was penetrated, he was feminized—his natural category was changed, so both he and the penetrator were guilty of "category confusion." The same principle of keeping categories distinct underlies other prohibitions, including some dietary laws and laws against crossbreeding animals, plowing with two different species of animals, planting different crops in the same field, wearing clothing woven from different kinds of yarn, and cross-dressing.[49] Informed as they are by the principle of keeping categories separate, these prohibitions are culture specific. It is arbitrary to assert on the basis of biblical authority that some of them, such as sex between men, are intrinsically wrong, whereas others, such as wearing clothing made from wool and linen, are not: the biblical writers themselves make no such distinction. Yet some contemporary moralists do, insisting that some divinely given prohibitions are eternally binding, while blithely ignoring other prohibitions also divinely given.

Because same-sex relationships are addressed elsewhere in the Bible, and especially because of their relevance today, we need to examine this particular type of "forbidden relationship" in detail.

SAME-SEX RELATIONSHIPS IN THE BIBLE

Homosexuality is a modern notion—the word is first used in the late nineteenth century. Likewise, sexual orientation, in contemporary understanding, is a recent construct: if we were to ask ancient persons about their sexual orientation, they would give us puzzled looks.[50] We should more properly speak of "homoeroticism," in the sense of same-sex sexual relationships, rather than impose our contemporary understanding on ancient texts.[51]

What does the Bible say about homoerotic relationships? Not very much, especially in comparison to offenses such as murder, theft, and adultery, and not as much as people think. Before we return to various prohibitions of such relationships, we will first look at some narratives in which it is claimed that such relationships are described.

David and Jonathan

Let us begin with two men some modern writers have identified as lovers, David and Jonathan. David, Israel's second king, is the most important human character in the Hebrew Bible after Moses. In part because of his prominence, tales clustered around him, as they did around King Arthur, George Washington, and other leaders of legend and history.

David became king of Israel when the first king, Saul, was killed. One purpose of narratives about David's early career is to explain how it was that David, rather than one of Saul's sons, succeeded him. The biblical writers and editors give several reasons. First, it was God's choice: Saul had proved unworthy, so God rejected him and chose David instead, confirming that choice with a secret anointing by the old prophet Samuel that paralleled a similar ceremony at the beginning of Saul's career.[52] Second, David was simply better: he killed the Philistine giant Goliath, the story went, when no one else in Saul's army could do so. (That this is legend, as well as propaganda, is evident from credit for the killing of Goliath having been transferred from an otherwise unknown warrior named Elhanan to

David.[53]) Third, Jonathan, Saul's oldest son and presumptive heir, had himself recognized David as king-in-waiting.

What precisely was the relationship between Jonathan and David? The text says that Jonathan loved David.[54] But does this mean that they were lovers? David seems to say so. In his lament for Saul and Jonathan, who had died in battle with the Philistines, Israel's enemies, he gives lyrical expression to his feelings for them.

> Saul and Jonathan, beloved and lovely,
>> in life and in death they were not separated.
> They were swifter than eagles,
>> they were stronger than lions....
> I grieve for you, my brother Jonathan,
>> you were very lovely to me:
> Your love for me was more wonderful than the love
>> of women.[55]

So David remembers his friend, whom he loved. But how did he love him?

We get some details in 1 Samuel 18 and 20. Shortly after the story of David killing Goliath, we are told: "Jonathan's soul was bound with David's, and he loved him as himself.... Then Jonathan and David made a covenant...and he [Jonathan] took off the robe he was wearing and gave it to David, along with his armor, his sword, his bow, and his belt."[56] Later, after Saul had made plans to kill David, having correctly recognized David's ambition to succeed him, Jonathan and David reaffirmed their commitment to each other, and when they met for the last time, "they kissed each other and they wept together."[57]

For modern readers, these scenes have erotic overtones, especially stripping off clothing and kissing. But was the relationship between David and Jonathan homoerotic? Erotic language is culturally specific, and what we may consider erotic may not have seemed so to ancient audiences. Sometimes a kiss is just a kiss: in biblical times, as in many cultures other than our own, kissing between males is a simple expression of affection, not necessarily sexual.[58] In societies in which women and men were segregated until marriage, and in which women were thought inferior to men, male bonding was commonplace. We find similar language used of other ancient male heroes, such as Gilgamesh and Enkidu in the popular Mesopotamian epic named after the former, and Achilles and Patroclus in the *Iliad*. None of these heroes were male homosexuals in the modern sense—men whose sexual urges were primarily for other men. As is also true of Gilgamesh and Achilles, there are several references to David's sexual interest in women—the Bathsheba episode is a prime example. So David knew what "the love of women" was,[59] and his speaking of Jonathan's love as "more wonderful" than it celebrates the very special nature of male friendships in patriarchal societies.

The word "love" has another dimension. Signers of ancient Near Eastern treaties were said to "love" each other and could call each other "brother" when they were political equals, and "father" or "son" when one was more powerful than the other. A good example is the treaty, or covenant—the Hebrew term *berît* is also used—between Hiram, the king of Tyre, and David, after he had become king, later renewed between Hiram and David's successor, Solomon. In this treaty, they referred to each other as "brothers" who "loved" each other.[60] The same conventional language, part of a semantic cluster having to do with covenant, is used of Jonathan and David. They had made a covenant according to which Jonathan had ceded to David his status as crown prince: that is why he gave him his royal garb. Like Hiram and David, Jonathan and David were covenant partners, "brothers" who loved each other, but despite the claims of some gay activists,[61] they were not sexual partners.

Sodom and Sodomy

Another supposed example of male homoeroticism in biblical narrative, often cited by modern opponents of homosexuality, is the story of Sodom, a proverbially wicked city. The precise location of Sodom and its sister city, Gomorrah, is unknown, but the biblical writers locate it in the region just east of the Dead Sea.

That region is the lowest on the landmass of the earth, more than 1,200 feet below sea level. Its geological situation and its elevation combine to make it desolate and barren. Temperatures in the summer can reach as high as 120 degrees, and whiffs of sulfur fill the air. How had this region become so forbidding? For the biblical writers, it must have been a divine punishment, for natural disasters, as well as disease and ultimately even death, were understood as inflicted by God. The story of Sodom's destruction is another example of etiology, a narrative explanation of the origin of a custom, social reality, or, as here, a geographical feature.

Sodom was where Abraham's nephew Lot had moved, when it was still "well watered, like Yahweh's garden, like the land of Egypt,"[62] while Abraham himself had stayed west of the Jordan River in the land of Canaan. But, the narrator informs us, "the men of Sodom were wicked, great sinners against Yahweh."[63] So great were their unspecified sins that, we are told a few chapters later, there was an "outcry"—a persistent complaint to Yahweh—and he decided to investigate. After his meal with Abraham during which he promised the birth of a son to Sarah, Yahweh informed Abraham that he was going to destroy the wicked cities of Sodom and Gomorrah "because the outcry against Sodom and Gomorrah is so great, and their sin is grave."[64] In an almost comical bargaining session, Abraham extracts from Yahweh the promise not to kill any innocent persons living in Sodom.[65] Then Yahweh's messengers (his "angels") proceed to Sodom to carry out their mission.

What was so grave a sin that would cause Yahweh to transform this fertile region into a barren landscape? As it continues, the narrative apparently gives a clue. The divine messengers are taken in by Abraham's nephew Lot, who shows them hospitality. After a banquet,

> before they lay down, the men of the city, the men of Sodom, surrounded the house, both young and old, all of them. They called to Lot, "Where are the men who came to you tonight? Send them out to us, so that we may know them."[66]

This is not just a wish to become better acquainted with the strangers in town, but, using a familiar euphemism, to "know" them.[67] Was sodomy the sin of Sodom? So it would seem. But wait—Lot then offers the townsfolk his daughters.

> Look—I have two daughters who have not known a man. I will send them out to you. Do to them whatever is good in your eyes, but do not do anything to these men, for they came under the shelter of my roof.[68]

As far as Lot was aware, then, the men of Sodom were not homosexuals, to use modern terminology: they would have been just as happy with Lot's virgin daughters as with his male guests.

In the end, the divine messengers saved the day,

blinding the citizens of Sodom, and the next day the city was destroyed, along with Gomorrah and its neighbors. Lot and his family, however, were saved, in fulfillment of the divine promise not to kill any good people in the city. (Lot's unnamed wife did not survive for long—she was turned into a pillar of salt for having disobeyed the angels' arbitrary command not to look back.) The implication, then, is that Lot had demonstrated his righteousness by his proper treatment of his visitors; offering his daughters to the mob was morally acceptable in such circumstances.

But what precisely was the sin of Sodom that provoked Yahweh to destroy it? The earliest interpretations of the Bible, chronologically and culturally closest to the times of the biblical writers, are found in the Bible itself. One such interpretation is found in a first-century BCE Jewish work known as the Wisdom of Solomon. Referring to the inhabitants of Sodom, its anonymous author says they "refused to receive strangers who came to them...and made their guests their slaves."[69] For this ancient writer, one sin of the citizens of Sodom was an appalling violation of a fundamental social principle of antiquity, hospitality: they wanted to rape strangers in town. Now rape, as feminists have convincingly argued, is a crime of violence rather than one of sex: that is, rape is a violent form of dominance that uses sex, not an inappropriately violent expression of libido. So, the attempt to rape Lot's visitors is an example of Sodom's immorality, because they wanted to violate hospitality with violence against strangers in town.

We find a reprise of the story of Sodom in the horrible narrative of the rape of the Levite's concubine, which has aptly been called a "text of terror."[70] Set in the time of the judges, at the end of the second millennium BCE, "when there was no king in Israel," the story begins with the marriage between an unnamed Levite who lived in the hills of Ephraim in central Israel and his secondary wife, also unnamed, who was from Bethlehem in Judah, a few miles south of Jerusalem. But she left her husband and returned to her father's house. After four months, her husband went to get her back, accompanied by a servant and a couple of donkeys. When he got to Bethlehem, his father-in-law greeted him warmly—perhaps there was hope for this marriage after all. For several days they partied together, and even though the Levite was ready to go back home, his father-in-law kept insisting that they stay another night. Finally, on the fifth day, after more partying, the Levite, his wife, and his servant started out toward his home, some twenty-five miles to the north. But it was late in the day, and as they approached Jerusalem, the servant suggested that they spend the night there. The Levite refused, because Jerusalem was "a foreign city"—it would remain Canaanite until David captured it—and said that they should go a couple of miles farther north, to the Israelite city of Gibeah.

When they arrived in Gibeah, the trio started to

camp out in the town square; their fellow Israelites showed no hospitality. But there was another Ephraimite in Gibeah, an old man who, returning from work in the field, saw them in the square and invited them into his house. Then, while they were relaxing over dinner,

> the men of the city, worthless men, surrounded the house, banging on the door. They said to the old man whose house it was, "Send out the man who came to your house so that we may know him." But the man whose house it was went out to them and said to them, "No, my brothers! Do not act wickedly toward this man who came to my house, and do not do this folly! Here are my virgin daughter and his wife: I will send them out. You may rape them, and do what is good in your eyes—but to the man who came to my house, do not do this deed of folly."[71]

As at Sodom, there are strangers in town. As at Sodom, they are taken in by a resident alien. As at Sodom, the men of the city surround the house where the guests are staying and demand that the Levite be sent out "so that we may know him." As at Sodom, the host appeals to the principle of hospitality. As at Sodom, the host offers two women as substitutes—in this case, his virgin daughter and the Levite's wife. Now, however, no angels come to the rescue.

> The men were unwilling to listen to him, so the Levite grabbed his wife and sent her out to them. They knew her, and they abused her all night, until

morning. And as dawn began to break, they let her go. So, in the early morning, the woman went and fell at the entrance of the house of the man where her lord was, until it was fully light.[72]

Notably, this is not a Canaanite city, like Sodom, but Gibeah, an Israelite town, whose inhabitants are as bad as those of Sodom, the literary parallel implies. And, as at Sodom, homoeroticism is not the essential element of the story. In fact, like the citizens of Sodom, those of Gibeah are rapists, willing to rape women as well as men, with brutal disregard for the principle of hospitality.

That principle was a central component of Israelites' covenantal obligation to each other—to love the neighbor, the fellow Israelite. The men of Gibeah had violated that core principle, which explains the Levite's reaction:

In the morning her lord got up and opened the doors of the house, preparing to continue his journey. There was his secondary wife, fallen at the entrance to the house, her hands on the threshold. He said to her: "Get up! We are going!" But there was no response. So he put her on his donkey and proceeded to go to his own place. When he got to his house, he took a knife, grabbed his wife, and cut her, limb from limb, into twelve pieces, and sent her to all the territory of Israel.[73]

There followed a war of retribution by the tribes of Israel against Gibeah, and ultimately against the entire tribe of

Benjamin to whose territory Gibeah belonged, because some of its members had committed "folly in Israel."[74]

We must pause to consider the fate of this poor woman. Why did she leave her husband? The text says that "she was promiscuous"; ancient and modern translators have softened this to "she became angry with him." Is there a backstory? As often in the Bible, we are not told. Perhaps the charge of infidelity is a male narrator's anticipatory justification for what her husband did. In any case, this is patriarchalism at its worst: a helpless woman sent out to be gang-raped in order to uphold the principle of hospitality toward a male guest. And while it is risky to read our sensibilities into a text from another culture, here perhaps we are justified in thinking that the story was as horrible for its ancient readers as it is for us, both because of the result, the punishment of the perpetrators, and because of the poignant picture of the victim, who somehow managed to get back to the house where her husband found her lying, "her hands on the threshold."

The interpretation of the sin of Sodom as inhospitality is also implied in words attributed to Jesus. In the context of giving instructions to his inner circle, the Twelve, about their itinerant ministry, he concludes:

> When you come to a city and they welcome you,
> eat what is set before you, and cure the sick there,
> and say to them, "God's kingdom has come near

to you." But when you come to a city and they do
not welcome you, go out into its squares and say,
"Even the dust of your city that sticks to us, we wipe
from our feet in protest against you. But know that
God's kingdom has come near." I say to you that it
will be more tolerable for Sodom on that day than
for that city.[75]

As in Genesis and in Judges, the issue is inhospitality,
which will be punished more severely than Sodom was
for the same offense.

So, the attempted rape of Lot's visitors is an example of what displeased Yahweh about Sodom. But mis-
treating strangers was not the only sin of Sodom.
According to the early sixth-century BCE prophet
Ezekiel, addressing Jerusalem: "This was the sin of
Sodom, your sister: pride! She and her daughter[-cities]
had abundance of bread and undisturbed tranquillity; yet she did not support the poor and the needy.
They haughtily committed abomination before me;
and so I removed them when I saw it."[76] Justice was
most owed to those on the margins of society—the
poor, widows and orphans, and strangers. Sodom had
failed, in other words, to provide for these least powerful persons. This was the reason for the "outcry,"
a word that elsewhere in the Bible refers to pleas
for divine help from those treated unjustly.[77] And
this was the reason for the divine punishment—
the destruction both of Sodom in the past, and,

according to Ezekiel, of Jerusalem in the near future.

Throughout the Bible, Sodom is a frequently used byword for Israel. The prophets repeatedly compare their Israelite audiences to the inhabitants of Sodom, as did the author of Judges 19 implicitly. Thus Isaiah, addressing his audience in Jerusalem in the late eighth century BCE, proclaims:

> Hear Yahweh's word, you leaders of Sodom!
>> Listen to the teaching of our god, you people
>> of Gomorrah!...
> Refrain from evil,
>> learn to do good:
> Seek justice, aid the oppressed,
>> give justice to the orphan, plead the widow's case.[78]

Informed by these ancient interpretations, we can now define the "grave sin" of Sodom: it was social injustice—mistreatment of the powerless. Among the latter were strangers, and the story of Lot in Genesis 19 provides a vivid illustration of how strangers were mistreated in Sodom, by being subject to rape. Homoeroticism is only secondarily relevant.[79]

The Bible may contain another interpretation of the sin of Sodom, as sodomy.[80] That possible interpretation is found in the short letter of Jude in the New Testament.[81] Its author reminds his audience of divine punishment of sinners in the past:

The Lord, who once saved a people from the land of Egypt, later destroyed those who did not believe. The angels, who did not respect their status, but left their own, appropriate homes, he has kept in eternal chains in darkness until the judgment of the great day. Likewise, Sodom and Gomorrah and the cities around them, which, in the same way as they [the angels], were promiscuous and went after other flesh.[82]

"Going after other flesh" could refer to the homo-erotic proclivities of Sodom and Gomorrah; if so, it is the only biblical text that does so explicitly.[83] But here the context suggests an alternate interpretation. The line about angels refers to the myth of how the "sons of God" had intercourse with human women,[84] transgressing the essential boundary between the divine and the human realms. The immediately following verse about Sodom and Gomorrah may interpret what happened there as a similar transgression, in the opposite direction. Just as the sin of the angels was to have sex with human women, the sin of the inhabitants of Sodom was wanting to have sex with the angels who were visiting Lot—they went after "other flesh," that is, the "flesh" (a euphemism) of angels, which was off-limits to mere mortals.[85] (Apparently they were expected to know that Lot's visitors were angels.) In this interpretation, the sin of the inhabitants of Sodom was not ordinary sodomy.

Rather, just like the angels, they were mixing categories. So, at the very least, the letter of Jude does not necessarily refer to the sin of Sodom as sodomy.

A biblically literate reader may object, however, that the Bible does mention sodomy, or at least sodomites. Not precisely: no such exact term derived from the name of the city of Sodom exists in either biblical Hebrew or biblical Greek. Rather, translators have used the term "sodomite" for several Hebrew and Greek words. Thus, the venerable King James Version of 1611 translates Deuteronomy 23.17–18 as follows:

> There shall be no whore of the daughters of Israel, nor a sodomite of the sons of Israel. Thou shalt not bring the hire of a whore, or the price of a dog, into the house of the LORD thy God for any vow: for even both these are abomination unto the LORD thy God.

A more literal translation is:

> There shall not be a holy woman among the daughters of Israel, and there shall not be a holy man among the sons of Israel. You shall not bring the wages of a prostitute and the hire of a dog into the house of Yahweh your God for any vow. For both of them are an abomination to Yahweh your God.

As my version shows, the words translated "whore" and "sodomite" by the King James Version are, except for their grammatical gender, the same word, which means "holy"; in the masculine form, it also occurs in several passages in the books of Kings, in all of which the King James Version also uses "sodomites."[86] But its meaning is far from clear. More recent translations[87] render both words as "temple prostitute" or "cult prostitute," interpreting the law as a prohibition of sacred prostitution, that is, rituals that included sexual intercourse in order to enhance fertility.

Since antiquity, sacred prostitution has been claimed to exist, but, significantly, only by outsiders when speaking of other cultures. The fifth-century BCE Greek historian Herodotus reports that it was practiced in Babylon, Roman historians attributed it to their enemies the Carthaginians, and early Christian writers attributed it to pagans. Modern scholars have continued this "Orientalism," repeatedly finding in the Bible evidence for ritual prostitution among the Canaanites (and translating accordingly), just as biblical writers attributed sexual aberrations to their own neighbors. But because no Babylonian, Canaanite, Carthaginian, or other sources coming from the cultures where sacred prostitution is alleged mention it, there is a growing consensus among scholars that it never took place.[88]

In the law quoted above, the word "holy" is likely a euphemism for prostitute.[89] The same word is used of Tamar, when she tricked her father-in-law, Judah, into impregnating her by posing as a prostitute (for which the ordinary word is also used), and no temple is mentioned in the narrative about her.[90] ("Dog" is apparently a derogatory term for "male prostitute.") These men and women were most likely ordinary prostitutes, some of whom may have solicited clients in places where many people gathered, such as temples. In any case, while the law in Deuteronomy prohibits dedication of male and female prostitutes' earnings as religious offerings, it does not specify what the gender of their clients was, and it has no explicit connection with either sodomy or Sodom. Such disagreement among translators and interpreters over the centuries shows how changes have occurred in our understanding not only of ancient languages and cultures but also of sexual orientation.

Prohibitions of Homoerotic Relations

Some English translations of the Bible also use the term "sodomite" in two passages of the New Testament, which we will examine shortly. Let us begin by returning to the two laws in Leviticus that prohibit homoerotic relations:

> You shall not lie with a male as with a woman. It is an abomination.[91]

> A man who lies with a male as one lies with a woman, both of them have committed an abomination. They shall be killed; their blood is upon them.[92]

These two laws, of which the second is an expanded variant of the first, are the only explicit references to male homoerotic relations in the Hebrew Bible.

Both laws occur within catalogs of prohibited sexual relationships: sex with women belonging to the same extended family, intercourse during menstruation, adultery, bestiality, and so on. Leviticus further states that these practices, these "abominations," were carried out by the Canaanites who had lived in the Promised Land before the Israelites.[93] In fact, however, other law codes from the ancient Near East have similar prohibitions, so these are widespread taboos. Once again the biblical writers are attributing to others sexual practices that they considered beyond the bounds. Or at least a few of those writers. The prohibition against male-on-male intercourse is not found in the laws of Deuteronomy, despite broad overlap between its laws and those found earlier in Exodus and Leviticus. Finally, the Hebrew Bible is silent about lesbian relationships, probably because they did not relate to patriarchy—or, for that matter, to paternity.

Like the Hebrew Bible, the New Testament says little about homoerotic relationships, but three passages do condemn them. The earliest is in a letter of Paul to the Christian community in the Greek city of Corinth.

Do you not know that wrongdoers will not inherit God's kingdom? Do not be deceived: neither

fornicators, nor idolaters, nor adulterers, nor soft
men, nor males who bed males, nor thieves, nor the
greedy, nor drunkards, nor the verbally abusive,
nor robbers will inherit God's kingdom. Yet some
of you were such. But you were washed, but you were
sanctified, but you were justified in the name of the
Lord Jesus Christ and in the spirit of our God.[94]

Here Paul is adapting a genre that was a favorite of
Greek and Roman moralists and of early Christian writers too—a list of virtues and vices. Among the vices he
catalogs are male homoerotic relationships, and probably the behavior connected with them.[95] That in general
is clear, although the words Paul uses are not, and translations may lead us astray. Other translators interpret
the word that I have translated literally as "soft men" to
mean "male prostitutes," "boy prostitutes," and "the
effeminate."[96] Likewise, the word that I have translated
"males who bed males" is translated variously as "practicing homosexuals," "sexual perverts," and "sodomites."[97]
Again, these translations tell us more about the translators' own views of same-sex relationships than what the
original Greek words mean.

The Greek word that I have translated "males who
bed males" is a rare one, and its earliest occurrence in
Greek literature is in 1 Corinthians. It seems to have
been coined by Paul on the basis of the ancient Greek
translation of Leviticus 18.22 and 20.13.[98] So, whatever

Paul may have known, or thought, of homoerotic relationships in Greek culture, here he seems to be informed by biblical law.

We find a similar list in 1 Timothy, a letter attributed to Paul but not written by him. In the context of a discussion about "the law" (the Torah), its author states:

> The law was not laid down for the just, but for the lawless and the unruly, the impious and the sinful, the unholy and the profane, for those who kill their fathers and their mothers, for murderers, fornicators, males who bed males, slave traders, liars, perjurers, and whatever else is opposed to sound teaching, according to the gospel of glory of the blessed God, with which I was entrusted.[99]

As in 1 Corinthians, "males who bed males" are associated with other criminals, as if their activity were evidently wrong. But, like Paul, the author of 1 Timothy does not elaborate. Were some early Christian writers opposed to homoerotic relationships between males? Yes. Was their opposition due to a horror at such practices in their Greco-Roman milieu, or by their prohibition in Leviticus, or both? We do not know.

The third passage in the New Testament that touches on same-sex relationships is in Paul's letter to the Romans, one of his latest. Speaking of divine anger at idolaters because they willfully refused to recognize God's presence in the created world, Paul states that God punished them:

> For this reason God gave them over to dishonorable passions: for their females exchanged natural intimacy for unnatural, just as their males, giving up natural intimacy with females, were burned up in their desire for each other, males with males acting disgracefully, and receiving the reward that was due for their error.[100]

These verses contain the only explicit reference in the Bible to female homoerotic relationships. Moreover, they state that homoeroticism among both men and women was a divinely imposed condition: men who have sex with men and women who have sex with women do so because God made them do it. Ironically, this is not very far from the modern view that sexual orientation is innate rather than chosen, although Paul would not have put it that way.

None of these passages elaborate on their condemnation of homoeroticism. I suspect that Paul was informed in part by the ancient Israelite taboo against mixing categories, a concept found elsewhere in his letters. He also seems to have had a view of what was "natural," but it too was culturally conditioned, as was his insistence that men should not wear their hair long because to do so was unnatural.[101]

Jesus and Same-Sex Relationships

So some early Christian writers condemned homoerotic relationships. But what of Jesus himself? As a relatively observant Jew, Jesus would probably not have approved of male homoerotic activity because of its condemnation in Leviticus. But note the "probably"—for the Gospels report no words of Jesus on this issue, and, for that matter, little on human sexuality in general. He seems to have been more concerned with interpersonal dynamics and with humans' relationship with God than with sexual mores. If the later addition to John's Gospel in which Jesus stops the execution of a woman found guilty of adultery[102] reflects Jesus's own views about capital punishment, Jesus would not have approved of the death penalty for males who slept together, despite Leviticus.

What about Jesus's own sex life? Again, the Gospels are silent, as they are about whether or not he was married. (It would, however, have been unusual for an adult Jewish male of his time to be unmarried.) To be sure, there are ambiguities that later writers have elaborated in wildly different ways. For example, Mary Magdalene was Jesus's lover, even his wife, and together they had children. Or he had a special attraction for young men, especially one of his followers, "the disciple whom Jesus loved,"[103] who, as the King James Version translates the Greek, "was leaning on Jesus's bosom" at the Last Supper.[104] Although some interpreters have detected sexual innuendo in these relationships, it is unlikely that the writers intended it. That imaginative speculation can arrive at such inconsistent scenarios speaks to the lack of evidence rather than to the likelihood of either.

Biblical writers were aware of same-sex relationships, and a few explicitly opposed them, or at least some of them. But the writers' understanding of such relationships, like their understanding of gender and slavery, was that of their own times. Contemporary moralists who argue that the Bible is opposed to homosexuality (or, better, homoeroticism) are correct, but when they appeal to the Bible's authority as a timeless and absolute moral code, they ignore the cultural contexts in which the Bible was written. Moreover, such moralists are selective in their use of biblical authority. Few who argue that homosexuality is wrong—to say nothing about incest, adultery, and bestiality—because the Bible says so, would enforce the death penalty for these offenses as the Bible also commands. Does the Bible, then, have any relevance in modern culture wars over sexual morality, and morality in general? This is an issue to which we will return.

CHAPTER 5

FOLLY IN ISRAEL

Rape and Prostitution

Artemisia Gentileschi, *Susanna and the Elders*, ca. 1610.

Attempted rape is the crime in what may be the earliest detective story in history, one of several additions to the book of Daniel.[1] The tale is set in Babylon among Jews who had been deported there in the early sixth century BCE, although Babylonians do not appear in the narrative.

The tale is named for Susanna, the beautiful and virtuous wife of a wealthy man, Joakim, who also does not figure in the story directly. Two wicked elders in the community, serving as judges, held court in Joakim's house. When the litigants left at noon, Susanna used to go for a walk in her husband's garden. Each of the elders became sexually obsessed with her. One day they said to each other, "Let us go home; it is time for lunch." But each separately planned to come back to leer at Susanna, and when they met at the garden and discovered their shared obsession, they began to plot to consummate it.

One hot day, Susanna decided to bathe in her garden instead of walking as usual. When she sent her maids for oil and lotions, the elders came from their hiding places and asked her to sleep with them. "If you refuse," they said, "then we will testify against you that there was a young man with you, and that is why you sent away your maids." Even though she knew it meant her death, Susanna refused, preferring the death penalty for adultery, of which she was innocent, to violation by actual adultery of the law of Moses that her parents had taught her.

Susanna screamed; the elders screamed; people came rushing into the garden, and the wicked elders made their false charge. The next day, as they held court, the elders ordered Susanna stripped, so that, the narrator tells us, they could satisfy their lust for her beauty. Because of their status in the community, they were believed and Susanna was sentenced to death. In response to Susanna's prayer to God protesting her innocence, just as she was about to be led off for stoning (as in Shirley Jackson's story "The Lottery," stoning was a communal action), God inspired a young man named Daniel, not previously introduced, who instructed the people to return to the courtroom because Susanna had been unjustly accused.

With Solomonic wisdom, Daniel separated the two dirty old men and asked each separately under what kind of tree the alleged adultery had taken place. When their answers were inconsistent, he accused them of perjury, and they were put to death by stoning as the law of Moses required.[2] At the happy outcome, all praised God.

This short tale is permeated with allusions to other biblical texts. The garden is called in Greek *paradeisos*, literally a "paradise," like the Garden of Eden. We are also reminded of the sexually charged garden imagery in the Song of Solomon. Like other heroines of Jewish literature of the Hellenistic period, Judith and Esther, Susanna is pious as well as beautiful. Like Bathsheba, Susanna while bathing is eyed by men in positions of power, and she is helpless to defend herself. Susanna is powerless in court as well: she never testifies in her own behalf. So although Susanna is praised for her virtue, the real hero is Daniel.

The English word "rape" has no exact equivalent in either ancient Hebrew or ancient Greek. In the Hebrew Bible, the vocabulary includes words that mean "take," "subdue," and "force," often used in combination to mean rape. Rape is not mentioned in the New Testament.

A few laws in the Bible address rape explicitly. One concerns a woman who is not engaged:

> If a man comes upon a girl, a virgin who is not engaged, seizes her and sleeps with her, and they are discovered, then the man who slept with her will give the girl's father fifty [shekels] of silver and she will become his wife. Because he forced her, he cannot divorce her during his life.[3]

In a variant law,[4] the woman was seduced rather than raped. But in both cases the damage is to the woman's father rather than to her, and the man is obliged to marry the woman he had deprived of her virginity; how that occurred is irrelevant. The principal difference between the two laws concerns divorce, which here is not permitted in cases of marriage after rape.

In Deuteronomy this law is preceded by one concerning sexual intercourse with a virgin who is engaged— that is, contractually bound to another man. Different fact patterns and punishments are provided for such a case:

> If there is a young girl, a virgin, who is already engaged to a man, and [another] man comes upon her in the city and sleeps with her, then you shall bring them both out to that city's gate and stone them to death: the girl because she did not cry out in the city, and the man because he forced the wife of his neighbor. So you will clear the evil from among you.
>
> But if the man came upon the engaged girl in the open country, and overpowered her and slept with her, then only the man who slept with her should be put to death. You should not do anything to the girl; she has not committed a capital crime. This case is like that of a man who rises up against his neighbor and murders him. For he came upon her in the open country; if the engaged girl had cried out, no one could come to her rescue.[5]

In this law, rape is a crime of violence: the parallel case cited is homicide. The only acknowledgment of the woman's rights is the presumption of innocence if she was raped where no one could have heard her cry for help; otherwise, she too is presumed guilty. The wronged party is not the woman but a man—in this case, her fiancé, whose "wife" has been "forced." A man had the right to expect his fiancée to be a virgin—in fact, presumably he had paid the bride-price for a virgin. Her loss of virginity was the equivalent of adultery. Again, how that occurred—whether by consensual sex, seduction, or rape—is not relevant.

Dinah

Jacob had twelve sons by four different wives, and many daughters as well. But the only one named in the Bible is Dinah, daughter of Jacob by Leah. While Dinah was socializing with the women of the area where her family was staying, she was raped by Shechem, the son of the ruler of the area: "He took her and he laid her and he forced her."[6] Afterward, attracted to her, he asked his father to arrange for him to marry her.

But Dinah's full brothers Simeon and Levi would have none of this, because Shechem had committed "folly in Israel" by "laying Jacob's daughter" and "defiling her." They took their revenge by pretending to agree to the marriage, on the condition that, as was customary in Jacob's family, all the males of Shechem's city become circumcised.[7] They agreed, and on the third day, while they were still in pain from the procedure, Simeon and Levi killed them all and removed Dinah from Shechem's house—the marriage, or at least the engagement, already having been contracted. Then all of Jacob's sons plundered the city and took captive the women and children, much to their father's regret: Jacob was worried about retaliation from other Canaanites. But Simeon and Levi said, "Should our sister be made a prostitute?"

This narrative informs us about attitudes toward rape. For Simeon and Levi, it was a "folly in Israel," a phrase also used in reference to the rape of the Levite's concubine.[8] Why were Simeon and Levi so outraged? Was it because of the rape alone? Jacob seems not to have cared about that: his daughter, although raped, would be married off satisfactorily, with full bride-price. For the brothers, it may also have had to do with the principle of endogamy, in which marriage was to take place only between members of the same group. The main issues, then, are tribal custom and family honor, not what happened to Dinah, whose own feelings are not described and who never speaks.

Shechem is also the name of the city where the episode took place. As often in Genesis, underlying the personalized narrative is a larger political issue—in this case, how the Israelites, descended from Jacob's sons, gained control over the important northern city of

Shechem. Later in Genesis, Simeon and Levi are condemned for their fierce anger, which explains why they lost power in Israel:[9] all the stories of the sons of Jacob ultimately explain tribal history.

Tamar

Named perhaps for her distant ancestor, Judah's daughter-in-law (it may have been a favorite name within the clan),[10] Tamar was one of David's daughters, whose sad story immediately follows the David and Bathsheba episode. This juxtaposition sharpens the reader's focus on issues of sex and violence in the royal court in Jerusalem. A beautiful and unmarried woman, Tamar was tricked into visiting her half brother Amnon (David had at least eight wives). When Amnon asked Tamar to sleep with him, she refused: "No, my brother! Do not force me! Such a thing is not done in Israel—do not do this folly!"[11] Instead, she suggested that he ask their father to give her to him as a wife. But he raped her. Afterward, unlike Shechem, he wanted no more to do with her, and sent her away. She left in tears, with ashes on her head and her royal garb—her "coat of many colors," like the one Jacob had given to his favorite son, Joseph—torn.

Amnon had violated his father David's rights by sleeping with David's virgin daughter, thereby diminishing her value. But as his oldest and favorite son, he went unpunished, while Tamar became a shamed and desolate woman in the house of Absalom, her full brother. Just as Dinah's full brothers Simeon and Levi killed the inhabitants of Shechem, Absalom himself killed Amnon, meting out the punishment that David was unwilling to exact.

The narrative about Amnon and Tamar is unusual in its attention to Tamar herself. In the story of the rape of Dinah, we are told nothing about her feelings and wishes. Still, even though there is some poignancy in Tamar's desperate pleas and in her situation after the rape, the social context for both Tamar and her brothers is patriarchal: what is at issue is the usurpation of a father's rights by his son, and when the father refuses to act, another son enforces the punishment.

For biblical writers, then, rape was like adultery: it violated the rights of the men under whose control the victims were—their fathers, brothers, fiancés, or husbands. What had happened to the raped women themselves was of minor significance.

PROSTITUTION

Not surprisingly, "the world's oldest profession" existed in biblical times, but we do not find it referred to in the Bible as often as translations indicate. The Hebrew root[12] rendered as "harlot," "whore," and "prostitute" often has a more general meaning, referring to a promiscuous woman not necessarily involved in sex for hire. An example is the prophet Hosea's wife Gomer, whom he married at divine instruction. She was promiscuous but probably not a prostitute, despite the misleading translation "wife of whoredom."[13] So while not all "harlots" in translations of the Bible were professional sex workers, there were some.

From texts scattered throughout the Bible we learn that, as in many cultures, prostitutes wore distinctive clothing[14] and perhaps head coverings as well.[15] They could offer their services either in houses, whether their own or brothels,[16] or at places where people gathered, such as city gates[17] and temples.[18] For their services, prostitutes would receive a "gift"—another euphemism—usually translated "wages" or "hire."

Prostitution is occasionally mentioned in biblical law. In the law in Deuteronomy discussed above,[19] the earnings of both male and female prostitutes were prohibited from use for sacred purposes, which suggests that prostitution was incompatible with ritual purity.[20] We find the issue of ritual purity in another law, which bans a man from pimping his daughter:

> You shall not defile your daughter by making her a prostitute; so that the land not become a prostitute and the land be full of depravity.[21]

Why would a father do this? Presumably for income—just as he could sell his daughter as a slave[22]—and probably an urgent need for income, rather than waiting for the bride-price when she married. Although such a daughter is called "defiled," the real issue is the purity of the land, the "holy land." Prostitution, then, had a religious stigma attached to it.[23]

Although Paul includes lists of vices, especially sexual vices, in his letters, those lists do not include prostitution. But after one of these lists occurs the only reference to prostitution in Paul's writings. The context is Paul's rejection of the opinion of some Christians at Corinth that, because they had attained a higher state of sanctity, they were not bound by the precepts of the law of Moses, whether these had to do with diet or sexual morality. Paul agrees that the dietary restrictions of the Torah do not apply to Gentile Christians, but he insists that sexual immorality is not permissible. He goes on to say that having sex with a prostitute is wrong because Christians collectively form the body of Christ, and as parts of that body they should not corrupt it by fornication, such as becoming "one flesh" with a prostitute.[24] His argument is essentially the same as that of Israelite law: prostitution is incompatible with the holy character of God's people.

In addition to laws, the Bible includes what scholars call "wisdom literature," whose focus is on the human condition. The books of Job and Ecclesiastes belong to this genre, as does the book of Proverbs, which is an anthology of sayings in poetic form that pithily and often cleverly articulate an aspect of experience. Such proverbs are another window into biblical views of morality alongside laws. Like adultery, the book of Proverbs asserts, for a man to frequent prostitutes is unwise, but for practical rather than religious reasons: "A man who gets involved with prostitutes will lose his wealth."[25] And, as foolish as prostitution is, it is not as bad as adultery:

> The cost of a woman who is a prostitute is only a
> loaf of bread,
> > but a man's wife will hunt for [your] precious
> > life.[26]

Significantly, prostitution here is the lesser vice—adultery, because it is a capital crime, is a much more serious offense. And in both cases the advice is given to men; no parallel warning is given to the women who might be prostituting themselves.

The first of several prostitutes to appear in biblical narrative is Tamar, the patriarch Judah's daughter-in-law, who posed as a prostitute to get Judah to fulfill his obligation to provide her with a son.[27] Thinking she was a prostitute, Judah had sex with her, and when her subsequent pregnancy became apparent, ordered her burned—not for prostitution but for adultery, because she was supposed to marry Judah's third son, Shelah. When Tamar disclosed that Judah had made her pregnant, he acknowledged that she had done nothing wrong. The narrative assumes that Judah's use of a prostitute was normal and acceptable, and Tamar has an honored place in the genealogy of David and thus of Jesus.[28]

The next prostitute mentioned in the Bible is Rahab. As the Israelites were poised to enter the land of Canaan after the Exodus from Egypt and the death of Moses, their leader Joshua sent two unnamed spies to Jericho, on the western bank of the Jordan River that the Israelites were about to cross. In Jericho, the spies went—immediately—to the house of a prostitute named Rahab, where they spent the night. Rahab is the first professional prostitute mentioned in the Bible. Why did the spies go to her "house"? Because it was an establishment where strangers in town would likely not be noticed? How did they know that she was a prostitute? Did she have a sign in front, or some other indication of the services to be bought there? Did they go to her house for the usual reasons? That is what the king of Jericho seemed to think, when he asked Rahab about the "men who went into you."[29]

Rahab had hidden them on her flat roof, among stalks of recently harvested flax. At night, when it was safe, she let them down through her window, and according to the terms of her agreement with them, she and her extended family were spared when Jericho's walls came tumbling down and its other inhabitants were slaughtered.

A traitor to her own people, Rahab saved the spies, and she and her kin became part of the people of Israel. Like other prostitutes in biblical narrative, Rahab is not condemned—on the contrary, she is praised throughout biblical and postbiblical tradition as a model believer. According to later Jewish tradition, she married

Joshua;[30] according to the Gospel of Matthew, she was the mother of Boaz, Ruth's second husband, and thus David's, and Jesus's, ancestor.[31]

Another prostitute was Jephthah's mother. His marginal status in his family is due to his mother's profession. As with Judah and Tamar, Jephthah's father Gilead's use of a prostitute is mentioned matter-of-factly, with no hint of disapproval, and his unnamed mother gets no further attention, but lurking in the narrative are familiar themes of sibling rivalry and the status of a secondary wife.[32]

The last of the judges in the book of Judges is the amoral strong man Samson, whose story on one level is an extended demonstration of his problems with women—unlucky in love as well as in life. Three women are Samson's sexual partners. The first is an unnamed Philistine woman, with whom he asked his parents to arrange a marriage for him. Although his parents initially objected because she was not an Israelite, the marriage was eventually contracted. At the wedding, in the Philistine city of Timnah, Samson bet members of the wedding party, some thirty men, that they could not solve this riddle:

> Out of the eater came something to eat;
> out of the strong came something sweet.[33]

The riddle itself, at a marriage feast, has sexual innuendo: it could be interpreted as referring to fellatio. But that is not the meaning Samson had in mind: he had earlier killed a lion, and when he passed by later a swarm of wild bees had settled in the carcass and made honey.

Unable to solve the riddle, the men threatened Samson's wife, and using her tears and nagging, she persuaded him to explain it to her. She passed the answer on to her fellow Philistines, who won the bet, saying:

> What is sweeter than honey?
> What is stronger than a lion?

Samson angrily retorted with another sexually charged verse:

> If you had not plowed with my heifer,
> you would not have found out my riddle.[34]

He paid off the bet, two fine garments for each of the thirty men, but returned to his father's house in rage. His wife, who typically had no say in the matter, was given to his best man.

Some time later, he went back to Timnah to "visit" his wife, but her father refused to let him see her, because she had married his best man. Instead, he offered Samson her younger sister: daughters, like those of Laban and Saul,[35] were fungible commodities. Samson took his revenge on the Philistines, burning their fields, vineyards, and orchards that were ready for harvest. They retaliated in kind, burning both his wife and her father and setting off in pursuit of Samson, who easily defeated them with the help of the "spirit of Yahweh."

Having learned nothing from this episode, the now wifeless Samson went to Gaza, another Philistine city, where he "went into" a prostitute. Again the Philistines tried to ambush him, and again Samson escaped. This nameless prostitute figures only briefly, and both her profession and Samson's use of her services are apparently normal social activities.

The third woman who got Samson into trouble was the notorious Delilah. Although not explicitly identified as a Philistine, she was on good terms with them, agreeing to ask Samson to reveal the secret of his strength in exchange for a huge amount of silver. Perhaps a bit wiser from his experience with his first wife, Samson three times gave Delilah false explanations. Finally, after days of nagging, he told her: the secret of his strength was his long hair, which he had solemnly vowed never to cut. So she caused him to fall asleep at her "knees," cut off his hair, and allowed the Philistines to capture him and blind him.

Poor Samson—one woman after another gets him into trouble. That is one of the morals of his story: women, especially foreign women, will do that. In the end, of course, Samson gets his revenge, bringing down the temple of their god Dagon on the Philistines and himself as they watched him entertain them.[36] This ancient equivalent of suicide bombing foreshadows the ultimate defeat of the Philistines by the Israelites under David early in his reign.

As a specific example of King Solomon's divinely

given wisdom, the book of Kings shows him hearing a legal case, as kings often did personally. Two prostitutes appeared before him with their story. They shared a room, and both had recently given birth. During the night, one of them rolled over onto her infant and smothered him to death. She took away the other woman's sleeping child and replaced it with her own dead one. In the morning the second woman discovered the dead child. Each woman asserted that the living child was hers and the dead one belonged to the other, and presented their claims to the king. To resolve the case, he ordered the living infant cut in two and each woman be given a half. The mother of the living child said that it would be better that the child should live, and be given to the other. But the mother of the dead child agreed with the royal plan. Immediately Solomon knew who the mother was, and he gave the infant to her.[37]

The centerpiece of the story is the Solomonic judgment; the status of the women as prostitutes is only of secondary importance. The narrative implies that they were living in an inn, perhaps even a brothel. Yet there is no condemnation of their profession, nor any indication that they are not Israelites.

Although Jesus is commonly thought to have associated with prostitutes, the text never says as much. "Tax collectors" and "sinners" were part of his following, and he shared meals with them, to the shock of some in his society, to whom such persons were socially unacceptable.[38]

According to Matthew, prostitutes were part of the following of John the Baptist, and Jesus is quoted as saying that they had a better chance of entering God's kingdom than the members of the religious establishment of his day.[39]

The frequent depiction in Christian art and literature of Mary Magdalene as a prostitute has no basis in the New Testament. She is conflated with the woman who washed Jesus's feet, but that woman is also identified only generically as a sinner, not as a prostitute.[40] So, although Jesus's entourage may have included prostitutes, who might be included under the designation "sinners," the Gospels never say so explicitly.

The only other prostitute in the New Testament is a symbolic one, "the great whore Babylon" in the book of Revelation. The symbolism draws on an earlier biblical metaphor in which cities were personified as women. Especially in the prophets, Jerusalem, the capital of Israel, and Israel more generally, are described as unfaithful and promiscuous spouses of the deity, and Nineveh, the Assyrian capital, and Tyre, the Phoenician port city, are called prostitutes.[41] In a vision the seer is shown "Babylon the great, the mother of whores,"[42] whom the original audience of the book would have understood to be not Babylon of earlier times, but Rome.

In biblical times, prostitution was part of social reality. It was disapproved of, but not explicitly because of its intrinsic immorality, and certainly not because it exploited women. For married men, having sex with prostitutes was not considered adultery, but it was discouraged in the book of Proverbs as wasteful. A priest's holiness was compromised either if he married a prostitute or if his daughter became one.

Most women who were prostitutes were apparently independent of direct male control. This may account for the absence of criticism of Judah, Joshua's spies, Jephthah's father, and Samson for their use of prostitutes: unlike in adultery and rape, there was no damage to a husband or father. The only hint of concern for women who were prostitutes in the Bible is the prohibition of fathers from exploiting their daughters as prostitutes. Yet even though prostitutes, like widows, were marginalized, they could also act heroically, as did Tamar and Rahab, quintessential prostitutes with hearts of gold. But negative connotations of prostitution dominate biblical tradition, especially in the metaphorical depiction of Israel, Yahweh's unfaithful wife, as a prostitute.

CHAPTER 6

FIRE IN THE DIVINE LOINS

God's Wives in Myth and Metaphor

An impression of a cylinder seal from northern Syria, ca. 1750–1650 BCE. The storm god, standing on two stylized mountains, is advancing toward a goddess, standing on a bull and opening her cloak to show her readiness for sex with her divine partner, the storm god on the left.

One of the exiles from Jerusalem to Babylonia in the early sixth century BCE was a priest, Ezekiel. There, "by the rivers of Babylon," he received a call to be a prophet too. In his Chagall-like description of the experience that inaugurates his career as a prophet, Ezekiel reports seeing "a vision of God."[1] It begins, as divine appearances often do, with a great storm cloud emitting fire. In the middle of the fire are four fantastic creatures; later the prophet will tell us that these are the cherubim, the guardian components of the divine throne.[2] Each creature has a wheel, its rim studded with eyes: these are the wheels of the "chariot of fire" that had carried the prophet Elijah into heaven more than two centuries earlier.[3] Over the creatures, on a crystal platform that they supported, was what seemed to be a sapphire throne, and on the throne sat a being with human form.

> And then I saw something with the color of amber, what seemed to be fire all around, moving up from what seemed to be his loins, and downward from what seemed to be his loins I saw what seemed to be fire.[4]

Piling up the qualifications and circumlocutions that permeate the prophet's account of his vision, the prophet concludes by explaining what he saw: "This was the appearance of the likeness of the glory of Yahweh."[5]

The vision has a surreal quality to it, perhaps to convey the ultimate indescribability of the divine presence. But why are the loins mentioned? In general, the loins are the area of the body, both male and female, between the waist and the thighs. When preparing for battle or flight, a man would "gird his loins"—pull up his garment and tie it around his thighs to allow his legs more freedom of motion. Because of their anatomical location, exposing the loins was shameful. The loins were also associated with reproduction: when a woman was in labor, her loins trembled. Using a vulgar double entendre, the Judean king Rehoboam is advised to boast of his superiority to his predecessor Solomon: "My little thing is thicker than my father's loins."[6] In Ezekiel's vision, Yahweh apparently has loins. Does this mean that he was a sexual being?

Many scholars in the past have asserted that he was not. Here are two statements that sum up the prevailing view:

- "The holy god of the Bible transcends sexuality (a point that became clear in the encounter between Yahwism and Canaanite religion)."[7]
- "God is not sexed, God does not model sexuality."[8]

But that view is derived from scholars' presuppositions about God rather than on what the Bible and other evidence indicates.

MYTH AND METAPHOR

All language about the divine is metaphor, explaining an ineffable reality in familiar terms. In the Bible, God is a king, a shepherd, a warrior—all elements of human experience and society projected onto the deity. Likewise, metaphorically at least, God has body parts: eyes, ears, heart, nose, arms, feet, even a backside, a rear end.[9] And, despite assertions that the god of Israel is not a sexual being, there are hints that he has reproductive organs as well, as in Ezekiel's vision.

This is hardly surprising. In mythology, which I would define briefly as the elaboration of metaphors concerning the divine, often in narrative and art, other gods and goddesses of the ancient world were sexually active. We have already glimpsed the remarkable "hand" of the Canaanite god El. Here is another example from Canaanite myth, describing the storm god Baal's sexual stamina:

He fell in love with a heifer in the desert pasture,
    a young cow in the fields on Death's shore:
he slept with her seventy-seven times,
        he mounted her eighty-eight times;
and she became pregnant,
        and she bore him a boy.

Egyptian and Mesopotamian texts are equally explicit. In one Egyptian myth, the creator god Atum, alone at the beginning, masturbates, generating from his semen Shu, the god of air, and Tefnut, the goddess of moisture. A Sumerian myth relates how the god Enlil raped the young goddess Ninlil, and the mixture of his semen and her blood produced the Tigris River. Many other examples are found in both the ancient Near East and the classical world. The biblical writers, to be sure, do not preserve such myths about Yahweh, but both in the Bible and in nonbiblical sources we find references to his sexual relationships and reproductive activities.

YAHWEH'S WIVES IN MYTH

Let us begin with the nonbiblical sources. The Bible gives an incomplete account of what the ancient Israelites and early Christians believed; important additional information comes from nonbiblical texts and archaeological discoveries. In the mid-1970s, at a remote site in the northern Sinai Peninsula called Kuntillet Ajrud, archaeologists excavated ruins of a caravanserai and fort that was also a kind of shrine. Several objects from the site, which is dated to the early eighth century BCE, were religious offerings, as inscriptions on some of them show:

> [May] Yahweh of Teman cause things to go well
>   [for him].
> Belonging to Obadiah son of Adnah. May he be
>   blessed by Yahweh.

Deep in the desert, worshippers of Yahweh prayed for his blessing, using standard formulas. But other, more remarkable, dedications were also found:

> I bless you by Yahweh of Teman and by his Asherah.
> I bless you by Yahweh of Samaria and by his Asherah.

The wording of these last two is the same, except for the place with which Yahweh is associated. Teman is one of the names for Yahweh's ancient home in northern Arabia, the likely location of Mount Sinai, where he first revealed his name to Moses in the burning bush, and from which he set out to lead his people to the Promised Land.[10] Samaria was the capital of the northern kingdom of Israel from the early ninth to the late eighth century BCE. Yahweh was worshipped in both of these places, and their names were included in his titles, much as in Roman Catholic tradition Mary, the mother of Jesus, is called Our Lady of Lourdes, Our Lady of Fatima, and Our Lady of Guadalupe.

The phrase "Yahweh and his Asherah" occurs several

more times in texts from Kuntillet Ajrud and another ancient Israelite site. Scholars do not agree on what it means. Asherah is a goddess who was the principal wife of the dominant god, and who was worshipped throughout the Levant, including in ancient Israel.[11] The Hebrew word *asherah* can also mean a wooden pillar, a stylized symbol of the goddess probably representing the tree of life. So the phrase "Yahweh and his Asherah" can mean either "Yahweh and his wooden pillar" or "Yahweh and his Asherah," that is, Yahweh and his divine wife. Either interpretation is heretical from the perspective of most biblical writers.

Drawing of graffiti on jar fragments from Kuntillet Ajrud.

One findspot of the phrase "Yahweh and his Asherah" is on a fragment of a large ceramic storage jar that was originally several feet high. On this jar were many graffiti, drawn by several hands at different times, as the drawing of joined fragments shown opposite illustrates. On the right is a seated figure plucking a stringed instrument; she is a woman, as shown by her dress, her hair, and her crudely stylized breasts. But she is facing away from the figures in the center, so she is probably not connected with them, any more than is the Egyptianizing image of a calf suckling its mother in the lower left.

The left figure in the center is a male deity; the headdress is typical of gods in ancient Near Eastern iconography. He also has bovine features, both ears and the tail between his legs alongside the phallus. The slightly smaller figure to the right is female—her breasts are similar to those of the woman in the chair.[12] This, then, is a divine couple. But who are they? Above them is an inscription in ancient Hebrew, which reads in part: "I bless you by Yahweh of Samaria and by his Asherah." The text may just be another graffito, but its position above the divine couple suggests that it is a caption. What we have, then, is a doubly illicit artifact. It violates the prohibition against making images of Yahweh, giving us a (less than flattering) picture of him. And it shows him arm in arm with his divine wife, the goddess Asherah. The graffito and the accompanying caption thus resolve the meaning of the phrase "Yahweh and his Asherah": it means the divine couple.

Judean fertility figurines.

Other archaeological evidence from ancient Israel includes literally hundreds of fertility figurines depicting a nude goddess and dating to the first half of the first millennium BCE: more than half of these are from Jerusalem itself. These data supplement the biblical text.

POLYTHEISM IN ANCIENT ISRAEL

The view that there is only one God developed relatively late in ancient Israel. We find the first unqualified statement of monotheism in a section of the book of Isaiah written in the second half of the sixth century BCE.[13] Prior to that, the existence of other gods was presumed, although the Israelites were supposed to worship only one, their god Yahweh. But of course they did not: their worship of other gods and goddesses is well documented in the pages of the Bible. The second commandment—"You shall have no other gods apart from me"[14]—prohibits such worship, implying that it must have been widespread, as do repeated descriptions and condemnations of polytheism elsewhere in the Bible.

The Israelites had worshipped other gods in Mesopotamia before coming to the land of Canaan in the first place, and in Egypt before returning to it.[15] They also continued to do so after they took possession of the land under Joshua's leadership, as a summary statement at the beginning of the book of Judges makes clear:

> Then the Israelites did what was evil in Yahweh's eyes and worshipped the Baals; and they abandoned Yahweh, the god of their fathers, who had brought them out of the land of Egypt; they went after other gods, from among the gods of the peoples surrounding them, and they bowed down to them; and they angered Yahweh. They abandoned Yahweh, and worshipped Baal and Astarte.[16]

Israelite religion was thus more diverse than the narrow ideal enshrined in the second commandment. Many biblical writers frequently used polytheistic concepts, depicting Yahweh as the head of a large pantheon whose members advised him and celebrated his accomplishments. This pantheon functioned, as in Mesopotamian and Greek religion, as a kind of divine council or assembly, under the rule of the high god. "God has taken his place in the divine council," says the psalmist, "in the midst of the gods he holds judgment."[17] Even Yahweh himself was not a monotheist—before the tenth plague that preceded the Exodus from Egypt, he boasted: "On all the gods of Egypt I will execute judgment."[18]

One of the members of the Israelite pantheon was Asherah. She was worshipped in the Temple in Jerusalem, where her statue was clothed with garments woven by women working in the Temple precincts.[19] She, or perhaps another goddess, was the "queen of heaven," whose worship the book of Jeremiah describes in some detail. The setting is in Egypt, among Judean refugees from the destruction of Jerusalem in 586 BCE.

Then all the men who were aware that their wives had been burning incense to other gods, and all the women who stood by, a great assembly, all the people who lived in Pathros in the land of Egypt, answered Jeremiah: "As for the word that you spoke to us in Yahweh's name, we will not listen to you. Instead, we will do everything that we have vowed, burn incense to the queen of heaven and pour out libations to her, just as we used to do, we and our fathers, our kings and our officials, in the towns of Judah and in the streets of Jerusalem. We used to have plenty of food, and were well, and saw no evil. But from the time we stopped burning incense to the queen of heaven and pouring out libations to her, we have lacked everything and have perished by the sword and by famine." And the women said, "Indeed we will go on burning incense offerings to the queen of heaven and pouring out libations to her. Do you think that we made cakes for her, marked with her image, and poured out libations to her without our husbands' knowledge?"[20]

There is logic to their argument: when they worshipped the queen of heaven, with offerings that included cakes depicting the goddess herself, probably in the nude, they prospered. But when, following Jeremiah's preaching, they stopped doing so, disaster struck. So now they were going to resume the worship of the goddess in order to improve their situation.

In Jerusalem and throughout the land, this goddess, the queen of heaven, was paired with Yahweh, the king of heaven. Both nonbiblical and biblical sources thus testify to Israelite worship of a goddess, who, as in the rest of the Near East, was coupled with the national god.

Gold amulet from ancient Ugarit, ca. thirteenth century BCE. A nude Canaanite goddess, standing on a lion, with an ibex in each hand and crossed snakes behind her waist. The background is a stylized starry sky, recalling the worship of the "queen of heaven."

Scholars sometimes use the term "popular religion" as a convenient tag for nonofficial forms of worship. But the term wrongly implies that only in their homes, villages, and towns did people stray from the supposedly pure form of Yahwism practiced in Jerusalem. As the response of the exiles in Egypt suggests, however, this was not the case: the kings and officials were as much involved in the worship of the queen of heaven as ordinary men and women, and in Jerusalem as well as in outlying towns. From time to time, reforming kings are reported to have cleansed both the Temple and the land of such forms of worship, often under the influence of prophets such as Jeremiah. Eventually that reform perspective became dominant and shaped the strict monotheism of Judaism and its offshoots, Christianity and Islam.

But for most of ancient Israel's history, such strict monotheism was not the norm. Worship of other gods and goddesses is repeatedly attested, and polytheism pervades biblical language. We find an example in the opening chapter of Genesis, in the account of the creation of humans. Each preceding creation is introduced by the formula "Let there be" or the like, but this time, to mark the importance of the occasion, God addresses his pantheon, his divine council: "Let us make humans in our image, according to our likeness." The narrator then goes on to say:

> So God [*elohim*] created humans in his image,
>> in the image of *elohim* he created them,
>> male and female he created them.[21]

The general principle here is that humans are modeled on God, almost genetically—just as later in Genesis, "Adam fathered [a son] in his likeness, according to his image."[22] But that abstract understanding immediately becomes concrete: humans are modeled on *elohim*, specifically in their sexual differences. The Hebrew word *elohim* is plural in form (like "cherubim" and "seraphim"), and is often used in the Bible with a plural meaning, "gods," as in the commandment "You shall have no other gods." For reasons not fully understood, it is also used, thousands of times, with a singular meaning—"God." In the first line above, the singular meaning is clear, because the verb and pronoun are also singular, but there is ambiguity in the second line. The traditional translation is "in the image of God he created them." This does not entirely make sense, since the last line speaks of "male and female," and God in the Bible is not androgynous but male.

An alternative is to understand *elohim* in the second line in its plural sense: humans are male and female in the image of the gods—because the gods are male and female, humans are as well. Which male and female deities are the model? Although the entire pantheon is a possibility, the divine couple, Yahweh and his goddess consort, are more likely.

YAHWEH'S CHILDREN

In the Christian creed, Jesus is the "only begotten son of the Father." But was he really his divine father's only child? No: the pantheon included other "sons of God," mentioned some half-dozen times in the Bible.[23] Because of the phrase's explicit polytheism, translators since antiquity have often demoted these divine offspring to angels or some vague "heavenly beings." But there is one passage where the polytheism cannot be so easily softened:

When humans began to multiply on the face of the ground, and daughters were born to them, the sons of God saw how beautiful the human daughters were; and they took wives for themselves of all that they chose. Then Yahweh said, "My breath shall not abide in humans forever, for they are flesh; their days shall be one hundred twenty years." The Nephilim were on the earth in those days—and also afterward—when the sons of God went into the human daughters, who bore children to them. These were the warriors of old, the men of renown.[24]

This fragment must have been part of a larger myth, which, as elsewhere in the ancient world, recalled how, long ago, the offspring of divine and human beings was a generation of heroes. The biblical writers preserved it because stories of beginnings traditionally included a time when intercourse between gods and humans occurred and produced superhuman children. The mythology is explicit, and some translations acknowledge it by phrases like "sons of God" or "sons of the gods"; others soften it (as all do when the phrase occurs elsewhere) with "divine beings" or "sons of heaven."[25]

Who were these sons of God with whom the biblical writers tantalize us? They were the offspring of the king and queen of heaven and thus members of the pantheon over which the divine couple presided.

Are these references to Yahweh, his wife, and their divine children just literary convention—as when Milton invokes the muse at the beginning of *Paradise Lost*? Or are they a residue of archaic thinking, as when we say that the sun rises and sets, even though we have known for centuries that the earth is not the center of the universe or even the solar system? I would argue that neither is the case. Rather, the language of a divine couple and their offspring stems from a living religious tradition in ancient Israel itself, for which we have documentation in the Bible, in its polemics and commandments. We also have evidence for this tradition in nonbiblical texts and artifacts, even though these are only sporadically attested because of the vagaries of preservation and discovery. The cumulative evidence, however, is continuous and undeniable: Yahweh is envisioned as a sexual being.

THE GODDESS WISDOM

We find further evidence of this living tradition in the figure of Wisdom as she is described in several passages. In the oldest, from the book of Proverbs, Wisdom lyrically recounts her origins:

> Yahweh created [or begot] me at the beginning of
>   his way,
>   before his deeds of old.
> Long ago I was formed,
>   first, even before earth.
> When there were no deeps I was born,
>   when there were no springs or sources of water.
> Before mountains were sunk in place,

before hills, I was born,
when he had not yet made earth and fields,
and the world's first lumps of soil.
When he set sky in place, I was there,
when he inscribed a circle on the face of Deep,
when he made firm clouds above,
when he strengthened the springs of Deep,
when he set a limit for the sea,
so that waters could not go beyond his command,
when he fixed earth's foundations,
then I was beside him, an artisan,
and I was his delight day after day,
making laughter before him constantly,
making laughter in the inhabited world,
and my delight was with humans.[26]

The word "making laughter" has a sexual connotation, an interpretation confirmed by other descriptions of Wisdom as God's sexual partner. We are told that she "lives with God"—a word that can mean cohabitation—and that "the Lord of all loves her."[27] The first-century CE Jewish philosopher Philo makes it explicit: "God is Wisdom's husband."[28] And no wonder: "She is more beautiful than the sun, more than every constellation of stars."[29] As God's wife, Wisdom is a member of his divine council, and, like other deities, she has built herself a house—a temple.[30] More than that, as her autobiographical hymn states, she is God's partner in creation.

The biblical and nonbiblical texts in which Wisdom is so described were written relatively late in the history of the formation of the biblical traditions, and they are literary rather than explicitly mythological. But in my view, they are not merely a kind of metaphysical conceit, in which "Wisdom" is simply the personification of an abstract quality given quasi-divine status, like "justice" or "liberty." Rather, the authors of these texts drew on the living tradition in ancient Israel that I have sketched. These authors daringly appropriated polytheistic mythology, an appropriation that orthodoxy quickly rejected, by demythologizing Wisdom and identifying her as just "the book of the covenant of the Most High God, the law that Moses commanded."[31] But this need to demythologize, to back off from the polytheism, also shows how pervasive was the belief that Yahweh had a wife.

As time went on and monotheism became the norm, the mythology of a divine couple was reinterpreted, softened, even suppressed, although in both Judaism and Christianity it continued, and continues, to exist. One example is the Christian formula for the parentage of Jesus: son of God, born of a virgin. In the Hellenistic world in which Christianity took root, myths of gods and humans having children were widespread. So Zeus in the form of a swan mated with Leda, a union that produced Helen of Troy—in William Butler Yeats's lyrical retelling:

> A shudder in the loins engenders there
> The broken wall, the burning roof and tower
> And Agamemnon dead.

In Christian tradition, Mary, the virgin, becomes pregnant by "the power of the Most High"[32] and gives birth to the son of God—such mythological language would not have seemed exceptional to men and women of the first-century Mediterranean world. Moreover, in Christian tradition, Mary appropriately is given the title "queen of heaven," because of her status both as the divine wife par excellence and as queen mother. In Mediterranean Christianity especially she also supplies the feminine element missing in a patriarchal religion focused on a patriarchal God.

YAHWEH'S WIVES IN METAPHOR

Biblical writers often characterize the relationship of Yahweh with the Israelites as covenantal. "Covenant" is a legal term originally meaning contract, and it is used in the Bible to refer to several types of contracts in ordinary life. When biblical writers call the bond between Yahweh and his people Israel a covenant, they have in mind such contracts. One such legal analogue is a treaty in which a lesser king is bound to absolute loyalty to a suzerain or emperor and prohibited from making treaties with other rulers. In the same way, the relationship between Israel and Yahweh is exclusive: "You shall have no other gods apart from me." The term "covenant" is also used in the Bible concerning marriage,[33] and, using this analogue, Israel is Yahweh's wife, to whom she owes absolute marital fidelity. The use of marriage as a metaphor to describe the relationship between Yahweh and Israel is further evidence for the notion that Yahweh had a wife.

The story of the metaphorical marriage between Yahweh and Israel is a love story, elaborated at length in the prophets Hosea, Jeremiah, and Ezekiel. It includes an engagement ceremony, in which Yahweh promises:

> I will betroth you to me forever;
> I will betroth you to me in righteousness and justice,
>   in steadfast love and in mercy;
> I will betroth you to me in faithfulness,
>   and you will know Yahweh.[34]

After the engagement came the wedding, in which Yahweh the bridegroom rejoiced over Israel his bride.[35] Naturally a honeymoon followed, when his loving bride Israel followed Yahweh in the wilderness, after the Exodus from Egypt.[36]

But the love story became a tragedy. Israel was an unfaithful, adulterous wife, worshipping other gods, and Yahweh responded in character: he is, as the Decalogue and related passages remind us, a "jealous god";[37] here he is a jealous, angry, even abusive husband. Several prophets focus on this tempestuous sequel, beginning with Hosea, who proclaims that Israel must stop her promiscuity, or Yahweh will "strip her naked ... in the sight of her lovers."[38] Jeremiah expands the theme, comparing Israel's sexual appetite to that of an animal in heat; in retaliation Yahweh will strike down her children and expose her genitals.[39] Chapters 16 and 23 in Ezekiel provide the fullest elaboration of the love story and its tragic sequel. These chapters are interrelated and extended allegories, describing Yahweh's marital history—first with Jerusalem, capital of the southern kingdom of Judah, and then with both Samaria, capital of the northern kingdom of Israel, and Jerusalem. The two chapters also contain some of the most shocking and sexually explicit language in the Bible, language that prudish translators have often toned down.

In Ezekiel 16, the first allegory, Yahweh recounts how he came upon Jerusalem as a baby girl, left to die in the open field. (Exposure of infant daughters was apparently practiced in ancient Israel, as in many other cultures.) He rescued her, although his care was less than complete: "I passed by you, and saw you wallowing in your blood, and I said, 'Live, and grow like a wild plant.'" Then, he says, "you grew up and produced the loveliest of ornaments: your breasts had developed and your [pubic] hair had sprouted, but you were still naked and nude." Then, he says, sometime later, "as I was passing by, I saw that you were old enough for making love, so I spread my cloak over you and covered your nakedness," as Boaz did for Ruth, and he entered into a solemn marriage covenant with her.

The divine husband treated his wife well, bestowing on her fine clothes, beautiful jewelry, and the best food, and she was famous for her beauty. They also had children together.[40] But she became promiscuous, and she even took her gold and silver jewelry, had it melted down and made into phallic images and used them as sex toys. Then, he continues, she built a platform. There, says Yahweh, "you opened your feet for every passerby," including the Egyptians, whose "flesh" was big, and "your juice poured forth." But she was not an ordinary prostitute, accepting payment for sex—rather, she was a nymphomaniac, paying her lovers.

The second allegory, in Ezekiel 23, uses similarly lurid, even pornographic language, only this time Yahweh is telling the story of his two wives—monogamy not yet a requirement, even for the deity—Samaria and Jerusalem, symbolically if unclearly named Oholah and Oholibah. As in chapter 16, the principal focus is on Jerusalem, and again the description of her promiscuity is detailed and explicit. She uncovered her nakedness, and prostituted herself to many, including the Egyptians, whose "flesh" was like that of donkeys and whose emission like that of stallions, as they squeezed her breasts and caressed her nipples.

Now this is allegory, and political allegory at that. Yahweh's people, obligated to exclusive loyalty to him as a vassal would be to a suzerain, as a wife would be to her husband, had worshipped other gods and made foreign alliances. For violating their covenant with him, and not trusting in his protection, they had to be punished. Writing in the turbulent days of the early sixth century BCE, Ezekiel anticipated the inevitable destruction of

Jerusalem by the Babylonians and their allies, and interpreted it as a deserved punishment inflicted by Yahweh. In the allegory, the unfaithful wife or wives are punished, brutally, by their divine husband.

> I will gather all your lovers...and I will uncover your nakedness to them.... They will tear down your platform.... They will strip off your clothes and take your beautiful ornaments and leave you naked and nude. They will bring up a mob against you, who will stone you and hack you with their swords.... So I will put a stop to your promiscuity, and you will not be paying for sex again. Then I will lay aside my jealous rage, I will become calm and not be upset anymore.[41]

When his fury has abated, Yahweh will pardon his wayward wife: "I will establish my covenant with you, and you will know that I am Yahweh."[42] The theme of restoration is also found in Jeremiah, where Yahweh promises that he will not be angry forever,[43] and in Hosea, where Yahweh says:

> I will seduce her,
>> and bring her to the wilderness,
>> and speak tenderly to her....
> And she will respond there as in the days of her youth,
>> as on the day that she came up from the land
>> of Egypt.[44]

The restoration is given detailed elaboration in the final chapters of Ezekiel, where the prophet speaks of divine mercy that will return Jerusalem to its former splendor. This is picked up in the New Testament, which speaks of "the new Jerusalem...prepared like a bride adorned for her husband."[45]

The metaphor of the covenant relationship between Yahweh and Israel as a marriage, especially in its elaboration in Ezekiel's allegories, informs our understanding of the mythical depiction of Yahweh as having one or more goddesses as wives. Was Yahweh a sexual being? Clearly so in the imagination of biblical writers, so also in ancient Israel more broadly and in later Judaism and Christianity, both in myth and in metaphor. The assertion that "God is not sexed" is a tendentious overstatement.

Problems with the Metaphor

A foundational principle of biblical law and ethics is the imitation of God: the Sabbath is to be observed in imitation of the divine rest, resident aliens and slaves are to be treated as God treated the Israelites when they themselves were aliens and slaves in Egypt, and the book of Leviticus repeatedly urges the Israelites to be holy as God is holy, just as Jesus commands mercy for the same reason. The same principle applies to God as husband. The punishment of God's unfaithful wife is not just a metaphor but a precedent and a warning: "So that all women may be instructed not to act promiscuously as you did,"[46] or else they too will be punished by their husbands as God punished

Jerusalem. Husbands, the implication is, can and should imitate God, and wives should learn from the allegory.

But what sort of a model is this? The prophets present us with a deity with fire in his loins who is an insanely jealous and abusive husband, subjecting his wife to gang rape and gang murder, as with the Levite's concubine in Gibeah. Yet unlike the Levite's concubine, no trace of sympathy is expressed for these wives of the deity. In considering divine sexuality, we are again faced with the issue of cultural differences that makes interpretation of the Bible so difficult. The world of the biblical writers, as Renita Weems puts it, was

> a world where [women's] rape and mutilation were normal, legitimate, and conventional ways for men to assert their power over women. It was a world where husbands had power over their wives to do with them whatever they wanted, where husbands forgave their wives' adultery, wives forgave their husbands' battery, and both lived happily ever after.[47]

The perspective of the biblical writers, and thus of the Bible as a whole, was patriarchal—sometimes, as in Ezekiel, even horribly so. Those writers were predominantly men, and passages such as Ezekiel 16 and 23 appeal to a prurient, voyeuristic male audience: Yahweh's naked wives in the allegory are being looked at by the reader.

To be sure, the description of God as Israel's husband is metaphorical—but so are all descriptions of

God; in fact, all theology is metaphor. I suggest that if we read biblical descriptions of God's sexuality as merely metaphorical, then should we not do the same for mythological accounts of other gods as well? Conversely, if we term nonbiblical sources as mythical, then should we not do the same for the Bible?

In any case, whether metaphor or myth, the biblical depictions of Yahweh as an insanely jealous and abusive husband are problematic. Can an individual believer or a community of believers, for whom the Bible is authoritative, dismiss these passages out of hand? Are only some parts of the Bible authoritative? If so, what criteria do such individuals and communities use to decide which ones? These questions have been asked repeatedly over the centuries, and they are especially urgent today, when the Bible is appealed to in support of all sorts of "family values," often in contradictory ways. Before addressing these questions, we must begin by reading the Bible on its own terms—what it meant to its original writers and audiences. That also means reading the entire Bible, in all its grandeur and complexity and horror, not privileging only those parts that say what we think it should say or what we want it to say. We should not use it just as an anthology of proof texts to be cherry-picked for scriptural support for preconceived conclusions.

CONCLUSION

The Bible is an artifact of the distant past that has shaped our culture in myriad ways, and it continues to do so for better and for worse. That past—that foreign country—is no longer our home, yet our ties to it are many. The Bible has shaped the beliefs and practices of Judaism and Christianity, has inspired writers, painters, musicians, and other creative artists, and has profoundly influenced Western philosophy, law, and politics. For some modern readers, the Bible remains just an artifact, rather like the Pyramids or the Parthenon, still looming over us, whose cultural importance cannot be denied. For such readers, its values are those of another age: its patriarchy, particularly, is no model for human conduct.

For readers who are believers, the Bible continues to be considered an authoritative guide. Yet, while upholding it as such, individuals and communities of faith today, as through the ages, have of necessity been selective—not just adopting, but adapting, modifying, and even rejecting some of its teachings. Such selectivity raises profound questions about the Bible's authority. Is it possible to maintain that the Bible is authoritative while ignoring many of its explicit commands? If the

Bible is an anthology of historically conditioned texts, how do these texts apply to later situations? On such contemporary social issues as the environment, genetic engineering, and abortion, the Bible says little or nothing. On others, such as the status of women and homosexuality, what it says is unacceptable to many. And very few would accept every biblical pronouncement as absolute and absolutely binding. The messy details of the Bible itself—especially its inner contradictions—and the subsequent history of the interpretation of the Bible and of how Jews and Christians over the ages have both used it and ignored it, require thinking of the Bible in a more nuanced way than simply as the literal word of God.

The Bible is one foundational text in American society. Another is the U.S. Constitution: it, too, is a historically conditioned text that reflects the values and understandings of its writers, the Framers. Almost from the beginning, the Constitution has been considered inadequate—hence the twenty-seven amendments, beginning with the Bill of Rights only shortly after the ratification of the Constitution itself. Unlike the Constitution, however, the Bible cannot be amended: once its contents had been decided upon in the early centuries of the Common Era, it became immutable.[1] Furthermore, again unlike the Constitution, the Bible was written not at one particular moment but over the course of many centuries. Yet through the long process of its formation, the Bible in effect often amended itself, and it has continued to be implicitly amended by communities that accept it as authoritative.

Interpreting the Constitution, like interpreting the Bible, also involves a kind of historical-critical scholarship. What did its words originally mean? What did the Framers intend? And how do those original senses apply—or not apply—to the changing circumstances of the American republic? Yet what a foundational text meant when it was written is not the only question that needs to be answered: we also have to determine what such a text means in the present. To do so requires ascertaining the ideals that underlie the text.

Justice Stephen Breyer has articulated this constitutional theory in *Active Liberty: Interpreting Our Democratic Constitution*.[2] For Breyer, the principle underlying the actual words of the Constitution is democratic self-government—what he calls "active liberty...the sharing of a nation's sovereign authority among its people."[3] That principle—that value—is ultimately more significant than the actual words or the intent of the Framers. So, Breyer argues, a judge should interpret the Constitution "in light of its own practical concern for an active liberty that is itself a practical process.... The Constitution authorizes courts to proceed 'practically' when they examine new laws in light of the Constitution's enduring values."[4] Thus, judges should not "rely too heavily upon just text and textual aids when interpreting a statute,"[5] but rather on what he calls the "framework" of the

Constitution, a framework that "assures each individual that the law will treat him or her with equal respect."[6] That principle led to amendments to the Constitution to abolish slavery and to give women the right to vote, positions that the Framers would have rejected unequivocally.

For both the Bible and the Constitution, social change often precedes the reinterpretation of the foundational text. The text itself is not the principal catalyst for change, but once a change is under way, the text is invoked (or, in the case of the Constitution, even amended) to support that change. Yet there is a paradoxical movement in the other direction as well. On the basis of their understandings of biblical teaching, or constitutional principles, or both, social reformers and political thinkers reach positions that later become mainstream. In other words, the foundational text paradoxically can serve as catalyst for change.

There is thus, as Archibald Cox has suggested, a dynamic rather than a static relationship between a community and its foundational text.[7] The text shapes the community—its beliefs, its values, and its practices. Yet, as society changes, neither the foundational text itself nor the precedents of interpretation are mechanically binding. Through the processes of expansion, modification, interpretation, reinterpretation, adaptation, selection, and even selective rejection, the community in a very real way shapes the text as well. The text is not, except perhaps in the abstract, intrinsically authoritative: it derives its authority from the community. And that community—or, in the case of the Bible, those communities—have a continuous and interrelated history that cumulatively provides authority both to the text and to the process of change.

As an illustration, let us consider a specific issue from the culture wars of another era, the issue of slavery. Every part of the Bible reflects the views of its writers, and for them all, from the early Israelites to the latest authors of the New Testament, slavery was divinely ordained and beyond question. Yet the biblical story and the laws embedded in it also imply an alternate, even subversive view. The formative experience for early Israel was the escape from slavery in Egypt. That experience is recalled at the beginning of the Decalogue: "I am Yahweh your God, who brought you out of the land of Egypt, out of the house of slaves."[8] The Exodus thus implicitly serves as motive for observance of the commandments—"This is what I did for you. Now I want you do to the following for me"—and is often recalled in the laws that follow: "You were a slave in the land of Egypt...you were aliens in the land of Egypt."[9] The repeated experience of liberation informs the interlocking histories of Judaism and Christianity as well as their scriptures. In one version of the Ten Commandments, Moses instructs the Israelites to observe the Sabbath, "so that your male and female slaves may rest like you. Remember that you were a slave in the land of Egypt and Yahweh your God brought you out of there."[10]

Implicit in these repeated references to the Exodus

from Egypt is the principle of imitation of God: if God had delivered the Israelites from slavery, then perhaps Jews and Christians should do the same for their own slaves. They should treat others as they themselves had been treated, and would wish to be treated. "Do not do to your neighbor what is hateful to you: this is the whole Torah; the rest is commentary," said Hillel, the famous rabbi of the late first century BCE.[11] His near contemporary, Rabbi Jesus, said much the same: "Whatever you wish people to do to you, so you should do to them: for this is the Law and the Prophets."[12] The essence of the scripture, then, is fair and equitable treatment of others; the actual words are not necessarily binding.

Hence, relying on the overarching authority of the Bible, rather than on the actual words of specific biblical writers for whom slavery was not only permissible but even divinely decreed, abolitionists argued that slavery should be ended because it was contrary to the essence of the biblical message. The same analysis can be applied to issues like the status of women and, I would argue, of any individual or group perceived as inferior.

One can thus trace a kind of trajectory from biblical times to the present and into the future. The trajectory moves toward the goal of freedom for all, in an inclusive community. This goal, this inspired ideal, is the underlying principle of the Bible—its subtext, as it were. Any specific biblical text is an incomplete formulation of the ideal because it is historically conditioned, and so it should not be taken as absolute in any sense. Moreover, no single biblical text adequately expresses the ideal, and in fact some texts clearly are counter to it from our perspective. Taken as a whole, however, the Bible can be understood as the record of the beginning of a continuous movement toward the goal of full freedom and equality for all persons, regardless of social status, gender, ethnicity, age, or sexual orientation.[13] How—and even if—a particular text speaks to an individual or a community in the present must be determined by testing it with the touchstone of fair and equal treatment of the neighbor, as seen in the strikingly similar sayings of Hillel and Jesus.

To put it somewhat differently, like the Constitution, biblical teachings have proven to be flexible, adaptable to new situations vastly different from their original contexts. Like the Constitution as well, the Bible must be interpreted—interpreted critically—to ensure that its underlying principle of love of neighbor in fact does apply. The principle is expressed in the book of Leviticus[14] and reiterated by Jesus[15] and his followers, such as Paul:

> "You shall not commit adultery," "You shall not murder," "You shall not steal," "You shall not covet," and every other commandment, are summed up in this saying: "Love your neighbor as yourself." Love does no wrong to a neighbor; therefore, love is the fulfilling of the law.[16]

This principle can and should continue to inform a society that aspires to "liberty and justice for all."

ACKNOWLEDGMENTS

In somewhat different form, parts of this book were lectures given at Oberlin College, High Point University, Huron University College, and annual seminars of the Biblical Archaeology Society, as well as to my students at Stonehill College and Harvard Divinity School. I thank all of these institutions for their willingness to let me try out some of my ideas at a preliminary stage.

I am grateful to friends and family members who read all or parts of this book in draft and who greatly helped me express myself more clearly: Kathleen Brandes, Thomas Cahill, Daniel Coogan, Elizabeth Coogan, Matthew Coogan, Michael Drons, Elizabeth Hill, Pamela Hill, and Christopher Horan.

I thank my friends Thomas Cahill, Bart Ehrman, and James Kugel, who encouraged me in this project at an early stage. I especially thank my agent, Stephen Hanselman, of LevelFiveMedia, and my editor, Jonathan Karp, of Twelve, for their encouragement and support.

ILLUSTRATION CREDITS

Chapter 1

P. 2: Gustav Klimt, *Adam and Eve*. Österreichische Galerie, Vienna.

Chapter 2

P. 20: *The Mirror of Human Salvation*. God, Adam, and Eve. Réunion des Musées Nationaux/Art Resource, NY.

Chapter 3

P. 62: Matthias Stomer, *Sarah Bringing Hagar to Abraham*. Gemaldegalerie, Berlin.

Chapter 4

P. 100: Hours of Marguerite de Coetivy. *Bathsheba Bathing*. Réunion des Musées Nationaux/Art Resource, NY.

Chapter 5

P. 142: Artemisia Gentileschi, *Susanna and the Elders*. Schloss Weissenstein, Pommersfelden.

Chapter 6

P. 162: Deities on North Syrian Seal. © Foundation BIBLE+ ORIENT, Freiburg, Switzerland.

P. 168: Kuntillet Ajrud. Zev Radovan/www.BibleLand Pictures.com.

P. 170: Pillar Figurines. David Harris.

P. 174: Canaanite Goddess. Réunion des Musées Nationaux/Art Resource, NY.

BIBLIOGRAPHY

Here are some of the scholarly works I have found helpful in writing this book.

General

Howard Eilberg-Schwartz, *God's Phallus and Other Problems for Men and Monotheism*. Boston: Beacon, 1994.

Carol Meyers, ed., *Women in Scripture: A Dictionary of Named and Unnamed Women in the Hebrew Bible, the Apocryphal/ Deuterocanonical Books, and the New Testament*. Boston: Houghton Mifflin, 2000.

Karel van der Toorn et al., eds., *Dictionary of Deities and Demons in the Bible*. Leiden: Brill, 2nd ed., 1999.

Chapter 1   To Know in the Biblical Sense: Speaking of Sex

John H. Elliott, "Deuteronomy—Shameful Encroachment on Shameful Parts: Deuteronomy 25:11–12 and Biblical Euphemism," pp. 161–76 in *Ancient Israel: The Old Testament in Its Social Context* (ed. Philip F. Esler; Minneapolis, MN: Fortress, 2006).

J. Cheryl Exum, *Song of Songs: A Commentary*. The Old Testament Library. Louisville, KY: Westminster John Knox, 2005.

Marvin H. Pope, *Song of Songs: A New Translation with Introduction and Commentary*. Anchor Bible 7C. Garden City, NY: Doubleday, 1977.

Stefan Schorch, *Euphemismen in der Hebräischen Bibel*. Wiesbaden: Harrassowitz, 2000.

Edward Ullendorff, "The Bawdy Bible," *Bulletin of the School of Oriental and African Studies* 42 (1979), 425–56.

Chapter 2 He Will Rule over You: The Status of Women

Phyllis A. Bird, *Missing Persons and Mistaken Identities: Women and Gender in Ancient Israel.* Minneapolis, MN: Fortress, 1997.

Cynthia R. Chapman, *The Gendered Language of Warfare in the Israelite-Assyrian Encounter.* Harvard Semitic Monographs 62. Winona Lake, IN: Eisenbrauns, 2004.

Hennie J. Marsman, *Women in Ugarit and Israel: Their Social and Religious Position in the Context of the Ancient Near East.* Leiden: Brill, 2003.

Chapter 4 Thou Shalt Not: Forbidden Sexual Relationships in the Bible

Susan Ackerman, *When Heroes Love: The Ambiguity of Eros in the Stories of Gilgamesh and David.* New York: Columbia University Press, 2005.

Bernadette J. Brooten, *Love between Women: Early Christian Responses to Female Homoeroticism.* Chicago: University of Chicago Press, 1996.

Stephanie Budin, *The Myth of Sacred Prostitution in Antiquity.* New York: Cambridge University Press, 2008.

Jacob Milgrom, *Leviticus.* Anchor Bible 3, 3A, 3B. New York: Doubleday, 1991–2000.

Saul M. Olyan, "'And with a Male You Shall Not Lie the Lying Down of a Woman': On the Meaning and Significance of Leviticus 18.22 and 20.13," *Journal of the History of Sexuality* 5 (1994), 179–206.

Chapter 5 Folly in Israel: Rape and Prostitution

Cheryl B. Anderson, *Women, Ideology, and Violence: Critical Theory and the Construction of Gender in the Book of the Covenant and the Deuteronomic Law.* London: T & T Clark, 2005.

Deborah L. Ellens, *Women in the Sex Texts of Leviticus and Deuteronomy: A Comparative Conceptual Analysis*. London: T & T Clark, 2008.

Hilary B. Lipka, *Sexual Transgression in the Hebrew Bible*. Sheffield, UK: Sheffield Phoenix Press, 2006.

Chapter 6   Fire in the Divine Loins: God's Wives in Myth and Metaphor

Gerlinde Baumann, *Love and Violence: Marriage as Metaphor for the Relationship between YHWH and Israel in the Prophetic Books*. Trans. Linda M. Maloney. Collegeville, MN: Liturgical, 2003 (2000).

Michael D. Coogan, "The Goddess Wisdom—'Where Can She Be Found?': Literary Reflexes of Popular Religion," *Ki Baruch Hu: Ancient Near Eastern, Biblical, and Judaic Studies in Honor of Baruch A. Levine* (ed. R. Chazan et al.; Winona Lake, IN: Eisenbrauns, 1999), 203–9.

Michael D. Coogan, "Canaanite Origins and Lineage: Reflections on the Religion of Ancient Israel," *Ancient Israelite Religion: Essays in Honor of Frank Moore Cross* (ed. P. D. Miller, Jr., P. D. Hanson, and S. D. McBride; Philadelphia: Fortress, 1987), 115–24.

Linda Day, "Rhetoric and Domestic Violence in Ezekiel 16," *Biblical Interpretation* 8 (2000), 205–30.

Peggy L. Day, "The Bitch Had It Coming to Her: Rhetoric and Interpretation in Ezekiel 16," *Biblical Interpretation* 8 (2000), 231–54.

Peggy L. Day, "Adulterous Jerusalem's Imagined Demise: Death of a Metaphor in Ezekiel XVI," *Vetus Testamentum* 50 (2000), 285–309.

William G. Dever, *Did God Have a Wife: Archaeology and Folk Religion in Ancient Israel*. Grand Rapids, MI: Eerdmans, 2005.

BIBLIOGRAPHY

Tikva Frymer-Kensky, *In the Wake of the Goddesses: Women, Culture and the Biblical Transformation of Pagan Myth*. New York: Free Press, 1992.

Judith Hadley, *The Cult of Asherah in Ancient Israel and Judah*. Cambridge: Cambridge University Press, 2000.

P. R. S. Moorey, *Idols of the People: Miniature Images of Clay in the Ancient Near East*. Oxford: Oxford University Press, 2003.

Saul M. Olyan, *Asherah and the Cult of Yahweh in Israel*. Atlanta, GA: Scholars, 1988.

Mark S. Smith, *The Memoirs of God: History, Memory, and the Experience of the Divine in Ancient Israel*. Minneapolis, MN: Fortress, 2004.

Mark S. Smith, *The Origins of Biblical Monotheism: Israel's Polytheistic Background and the Ugaritic Texts*. New York: Oxford University Press, 2001.

Gail Corrington Streete, *The Strange Woman: Power and Sex in the Bible*. Louisville, KY: Westminster John Knox, 1997.

Renita J. Weems, *Battered Love: Marriage, Sex, and Violence in the Hebrew Prophets*. Minneapolis, MN: Fortress, 1995.

Conclusion

Stephen Breyer, *Active Liberty: Interpreting Our Democratic Constitution*. New York: Vintage, 2006 (2005).

Michael D. Coogan, "The Great Gulf between Scholars and the Pew," *Bible Review* 10.3 (June 1994), 44–48, 55.

Archibald Cox, *The Court and the Constitution*. Boston: Houghton Mifflin, 1987.

NOTES

Following current scholarly practice, I use the abbreviations BCE (Before the Common Era) and CE (Common Era) for the older BC and AD. I also sometimes use the "Hebrew Bible" to refer to the canonical Bible of Judaism, in preference to the more explicitly Christian "Old Testament."

Chapter and verse numbers occasionally vary in Bibles. Here I follow those used in the New Revised Standard Version, which at times are slightly different from those in the New Jewish Publication Society translation.

Unless otherwise noted, all translations of ancient texts are my own.

Introduction
1. http://www.gallup. com/poll/6217/Word-BibleBuying .aspx.
2. http://www.elca.org/~/media/Files/Who%20We%20 Are/Office%20of%20the%20Secretary/Assembly/ 082109_LegisUpdate.pdf.
3. *The New York Times*, August 21, 2009.
4. *Goodridge vs. Department of Public Health*, 798 N.E.2d 941 (Mass. 2003).
5. Using the words attributed to Jesus in Matthew 19.4; Mark 10.6.

6. Jeremiah 36.4, 32.

7. 1 Corinthians 16.21.

8. Numbers 21.14.

9. See 1 Corinthians 5.9; 2 Corinthians 7.8.

10. Exodus 20.5; Deuteronomy 5.9.

11. Ezekiel 18.20.

12. Song of Solomon 8.6.

Chapter 1   To Know in the Biblical Sense: Speaking of Sex

1. London: Hamilton, 1953.

2. Song of Solomon 4.1–7.

3. The rare Hebrew word may mean "navel" or "vulva." I have chosen "hollow" because of its ambiguity. Marvin Pope prefers "vulva" because the description is moving upward, and as he observes, "navels are not notable for their capacity to store or dispense moisture" (Marvin H. Pope, *Song of Songs: A New Translation with Introduction and Commentary* [Anchor Bible 7C; Garden City, NY: Doubleday, 1977], 617–18).

4. Song of Solomon 7.1–5.

5. Song of Solomon 5.10–16.

6. Genesis 4.1.

7. Numbers 31.17–18, 35; see also Judges 21.12 and compare Deuteronomy 21.10–14.

8. Amos 3.2.

9. 2 Samuel 19.33–35.

10. Proverbs 30.20.

11. Genesis 30.15–16.

12. Joshua 2.1–3.

13. Leviticus 18.6–19. See further pp. 108–9.

14. Deuteronomy 28.57.

15. Isaiah 7.20.

16. Ruth 3.7–14.

17. Judges 4.17–22.
18. Judges 5.27.
19. Genesis 32.22–32.
20. Exodus 11.5.
21. Exodus 4.25–26.
22. Others that are euphemistic are Deuteronomy 28.57; Judges 3.24; 1 Samuel 24.3; Isaiah 6.2.
23. Isaiah 52.7.
24. Luke 7.38.
25. Hebrew *yad*.
26. Hebrew *kap*.
27. Rule of the Community (1QS) Col. 7, lines 13–14.
28. Isaiah 57.8.
29. Suggested to me by Matthew Coogan; note King James Version's "remembrance" and compare New American Bible's "indecent symbol." The Hebrew word is *zikkaron*.
30. Joshua 2.3.
31. Ezekiel 16.26; 23.20.
32. Song of Solomon 5.2–6.
33. The only possible exception is 8.6, where the last syllable of a rare word (*shalhebetyah*) is understood by some scholars to be an abbreviated form of the divine name Yahweh.

Chapter 2   He Will Rule over You: The Status of Women
1. Genesis 1.27.
2. Genesis 3.16. The word translated "man" can also mean "mate," and is used both of animals, as in Genesis 7.2–3, and of human males. In the latter case it can be translated "husband," but that is not necessarily accurate here, because the couple has not been formally married.
3. Genesis 5.6–8. "Fathered" is how the English Standard Version modernizes the King James Version's "begat."

4. Genesis 11.26.
5. Leviticus 27.3–7.
6. Genesis 18.12. The Hebrew word is *'adon*; see also Judges 19.26; Amos 4.1; Psalm 45.11.
7. Genesis 20.3. The Hebrew word is *ba'al*; see also Exodus 21.3, 22; Deuteronomy 22.22; 24.4; 2 Samuel 11.26; Joel 1.8; Proverbs 12.4; 31.11, 23, 28; Esther 1.17, 20.
8. Isaiah 1.3.
9. 1 Peter 3.1, 6.
10. Numbers 30.3–15.
11. Exodus 21.7–11.
12. Exodus 22.16–17.
13. Psalm 68.5.
14. 1 Kings 17.8–24.
15. Matthew 14.13–21; 15.32–39; Mark 6.30–44; 8.1–10; Luke 9.10–17; John 6.1–14.
16. Luke 7.11–17.
17. Genesis 24.16.
18. Sirach 42.9–12.
19. Judges 11.1–3.
20. Judges 11.7.
21. Judges 11.30–31.
22. Judges 11.35–39.
23. 1 Kings 16.34.
24. Joshua 6.26.
25. See Exodus 13.13; Numbers 3.46–47; and pp. 23–24 above.
26. Genesis 22.1–19.
27. Genesis 18.23–33.
28. See, for example, 1 Corinthians 5.7; Ephesians 5.2; Hebrews 9.11–14; 1 John 4.10.
29. 1 Samuel 12.8–11; Hebrews 11.32.
30. 2 Esdras 16.33. See also Isaiah 4.1.

31. 1 Corinthians 7.8–9. Despite its resonance, the King James Version translation of the last phrase, "it is better to marry than to burn," wrongly suggests eternal punishment with hellfire, imagery that Paul does not use.

32. 1 Corinthians 7.32–34.

33. 1 Corinthians 7.25–26, 31.

34. Matthew 19.12.

35. I use the traditional names of the evangelists, although it is unlikely that any of the Gospels were written by the individuals to whom they are attributed.

36. Luke 7.33–34.

37. Revelation 14.4.

38. Not all, to be sure. Married Anglican clergy who convert to Roman Catholicism are permitted both to function as priests and to remain married, divorce being out of the question.

39. Luke 1.17. On the entire unit Luke 1.5–25, compare Genesis 15.1–6; 16; 17.15–22; 18.9–14; Judges 13.2–5; and see further pp. 73–75.

40. Luke 1.26–38; Matthew 1.18–25.

41. Matthew 1.20; 2.13, 19, 22; compare Genesis 37.5–11, 19; 42.9.

42. See John 1.46.

43. Romans 1.3.

44. Matthew 1.25.

45. Mark 3.31; 6.3; and parallels; John 2.12; 7.3–10; Acts 1.14; Galatians 1.19. Sometimes the brothers and sisters of Jesus are identified as his stepsiblings, born to Joseph in an earlier marriage; after their mother, his first wife, died, he married Mary. This fictional elaboration was developed to reconcile the repeated New Testament references to Jesus's siblings with the postbiblical doctrine of Mary's perpetual virginity. An alternate

explanation, that they were his cousins, is equally
without basis.

46. Judges 11.39–40.
47. Judges 5.1–31; see especially verses 1 and 12.
48. 1 Samuel 18.6–7.
49. See Judges 21.20–21.
50. Jeremiah 44.19. See further pp. 172–73.
51. Exodus 22.18; see also Leviticus 20.27; Deuteronomy
    18.9–14.
52. 1 Samuel 28.
53. Exodus 15.20–21. On the basis of 15.1, until recently the
    hymn was called the Song of Moses, implying that
    Moses was its author. But the text does not say this, and
    in 15.21 Miriam is clearly the author.
54. Numbers 12.
55. Micah 6.4.
56. 2 Kings 22.14–20; 23.29–30.
57. Nehemiah 6.14.
58. Isaiah 8.1–4. His name means "quickly the booty,
    hastily the spoil," a symbolic assurance of Judah's
    victory over the Assyrians, but a challenging moniker
    for a child to have. It is likely that another boy with a
    symbolic name, Immanuel (which means "God is with
    us"), was Maher-shalal-hash-baz's brother; see Isaiah
    7.14. The prophet Hosea's children had similarly
    challenging symbolic names; see Hosea 1.4–9.
59. See, for example, Ezekiel 13.17; Joel 2.28.
60. 2 Samuel 14.1–24.
61. 2 Samuel 20.
62. Luke 2.25–38.
63. Acts 21.9.
64. 1 Corinthians 11.5; Revelation 2.20.
65. Judges 4.6–10; 5.12.

66. Judges 4.17–22; 5.24–27.
67. Judith 12.10–13.20.
68. 1 Kings 21.
69. 1 Kings 18.19.
70. 1 Kings 15.13.
71. 2 Kings 11; see also 2 Chronicles 23.17.
72. Colossians 4.15.
73. Romans 16.7.
74. Philippians 4.2–3.
75. Romans 16.1–2.
76. Acts 6.1–6.
77. Luke 8.2–3.
78. Proverbs 31.10–31.
79. Exodus 20.12; Deuteronomy 5.16. See also Exodus
    21.15, 17.
80. 1 Samuel 25.
81. Galatians 3.28.
82. Sirach 44.1–50.24.
83. 1 Corinthians 14.33–35.
84. 1 Timothy 2.11–14.
85. Matthew 28.1; Mark 16.1–2; Luke 24.10; John 20.1. Mary
    Magdalene is named in all four Gospels. Matthew,
    Mark, and Luke also mention Mary the mother of
    James and Joseph. Mark also names Salome, and Luke
    mentions Joanna and other women. The discrepancies
    suggest that no great significance was attached to the
    women's role in the discovery of the tomb; see further
    p. 58.
86. 1 Corinthians 15.3–7.
87. Song of Solomon 7.10.
88. Genesis 3.16–19.
89. 1 Corinthians 11.3, 9.
90. Jimmy Carter, *The Observer*, Sunday 12 July 2009.

(http://www.guardian. co.uk/commentisfree/2009/
jul/12/jimmy-carter-womens-rights-equality).

Chapter 3   As It Was in the Beginning?: Marriage and Divorce

1. 1 Corinthians 13.
2. Psalm 127.3–5.
3. Psalm 128.3, 6. Here, in line with its tendency to use inclusive language, the New Revised Standard Version translates the Hebrew word for "sons" as "children," although not in the previous text.
4. The only exception is the case of Onan; see p. 110.
5. Some take the Greek word *pharmakeia* (Galatians 5.20; Revelation 9.21; 18.23; see also 21.8; 22.15) to mean a drug used as an abortifacient. But the common interpretation of that word as sorcery is correct. To be sure, like other ritual specialists in antiquity, sorcerers were often medical practitioners. But even if the word in the New Testament suggests the use of drugs, there is no evidence that it specifically has to do with abortion.
6. Exodus 21.22–25.
7. The same general statement is found in Leviticus 24.17–21 and Deuteronomy 19.16–21; see also Matthew 5.38–42.
8. See 2 Kings 8.12; 15.16; Amos 1.13.
9. Hosea 13.16.
10. Numbers 5.20–22, 27. She may also suffer a prolapsed uterus, so that she will be unable to become pregnant again.
11. Job 31.15.
12. Job 10.8–11, 18. See also Psalm 139.13–16. Also often cited in this connection is Jeremiah 1.5, but that is specific to the prophet rather than a general statement about all

fetuses; Galatians 1.15, based on Jeremiah 1.5, is similarly specific. In Isaiah 44.2 the same language is used metaphorically of Israel. In Luke 1.39–44, the stirring of John the Baptist in his mother Elizabeth's womb when Mary comes to visit is interpreted by Elizabeth as her unborn son's joyful recognition of Jesus, also still in utero. But for Luke that is a narrative device, and in his Gospel in fact the only time John and Jesus meet.

13. Laban conducts the initial negotiations, probably because he was Rebekah's full brother. Her father, Bethuel, participates only at the end.

14. Genesis 24.

15. Genesis 34.4–12. This took place after Dinah had been raped by Shechem (see pp. 147–49), and the marriage never took place.

16. Genesis 29.15–30; Exodus 2.21; 1 Samuel 18.17–27.

17. As in Genesis 24.65.

18. Hosea 3.2. Some ancient texts do not include the wine.

19. Leviticus 27.4.

20. Ezekiel 16.8; Malachi 2.14; Proverbs 2.17. The Bible does not mention written marriage contracts, but nonbiblical sources do, and the stipulation that in divorce the wife be given a certificate (see Deuteronomy 24.1; Isaiah 50.1; and pp. 85–86 above) suggests that in literate times there would also have been a written marriage contract.

21. Deuteronomy 22.23–27.

22. Tobit 4.12.

23. Genesis 21.21.

24. Genesis 28.2. Rebekah herself wanted the same outcome; see Genesis 27.46.

25. Deuteronomy 7.3–4; see also Exodus 34.16.

26. 1 Kings 16.31–32; 18.19; 21.25.

27. Genesis 38.2.

28. Genesis 41.50. This marriage is the subject of a postbiblical work, *Joseph and Asenath.* It tells how Asenath was unwilling to marry the man her father had chosen, Joseph—after all, he was a foreigner. But she fell in love with him when she saw how handsome he was. For his part, Joseph would not marry Asenath until she converted, which she duly did.

29. Ruth 4.13–22.

30. Moses's wife Zipporah was a Midianite (Exodus 2.16–21). Later the text calls his wife a Cushite, which could refer to a second wife. However, Cush is not only a name for Ethiopia, but also a poetic equivalent for Midian (see Habakkuk 3.7), so it is more likely that there was only one wife.

31. Numbers 12.1–2.

32. Esther, Addition C, v. 26 (sometimes numbered 14.15).

33. Judges 13.2–24.

34. 1 Samuel 1.1–20.

35. Luke 1.5–24.

36. Genesis 16.1–4.

37. Genesis 16.4–6; see also Proverbs 30.23.

38. Genesis 18.1–14.

39. Genesis 18.12–15.

40. Genesis 21.6.

41. Genesis 26.6–9; compare Genesis 12.11–12; 20.2; and see pp. 112–13.

42. Genesis 26:8 in King James Version; New Jewish Publication Society Translation, New Revised Standard Version, New American Bible; Revised English Bible, New International Version.

43. New English Bible.

44. The same connotation is present in the story of the Golden Calf (itself a very complicated narrative). After

the calf had been made, on the day of the festival (to Yahweh), the people offered sacrifices, and then "sat down to eat and drink and got up to make laughter" (Exodus 32.6)—implying that not only was idolatry involved, but also an orgy.

45. Genesis 21.9–10.

46. Genesis 30.1–13.

47. Genesis 25.1–2. Like Jacob, both Ishmael (Genesis 17.20) and Nahor (Genesis 22.20–24) each had twelve sons.

48. Judith and Basemath (Genesis 26.34); Mahalath (Genesis 28.9); and Adah and Oholibamah (Genesis 36.1).

49. Judges 8.30.

50. Hannah and Peninnah (1 Samuel 1.2).

51. In the Bible the latest men reported to have more than one wife are the last two kings of Judah, in the early sixth century BCE, Jehoiachin (2 Kings 24.15) and Zedekiah (Jeremiah 38.23). In the same period two allegorical wives are attributed to Yahweh by the prophet Ezekiel (23.4); see further pp. 183–84. Biblical laws also attest to the practice, as does the late third-century BCE writer Ben Sira (26.6; 37.11), who may be quoting older proverbs. For the later evidence, see R. Katzoff, "Polygamy in P. Yadin?" *Zeitschrift für Papyrologie und Epigraphik* 109 (1995), 128–32; and S. Lowy, "The Extent of Jewish Polygamy in Talmudic Times," *Journal of Jewish Studies* 9 (1958), 115–38.

52. In postbiblical tradition Adam had a wife before Eve, the notorious Lilith, who left him, medieval legend says, because when they made love he refused to let her be on top. Banished from Eden, she became a night demon, and more recently has become a kind of patron saint of Jewish feminists.

53. Genesis 4.19.
54. Deuteronomy 21.15–17. For a different take, see Proverbs 30.23.
55. Michal (1 Samuel 18.27); Ahinoam, Abigail, Maacah, Haggith, Abital, Eglah (2 Samuel 2.2; 3.2–5); Bathsheba (2 Samuel 11.27; see further pp. 104–8). For the concubines, see 2 Samuel 16.21–22; 1 Kings 1.2–4.
56. 1 Kings 11.3; see also Song of Solomon 6.8.
57. 1 Kings 11.1–13; see also Deuteronomy 17.17.
58. 2 Samuel 3.6–11.
59. 2 Samuel 12.8.
60. 2 Samuel 16.20–22.
61. 1 Kings 1.1–4.
62. 1 Kings 2.13–25.
63. See Mordechai Cogan, *The Raging Torrent: Historical Inscriptions from Assyria and Babylonia Relating to Ancient Israel* (Jerusalem: Carta, 2008), 115.
64. Jeremiah 8.10.
65. John 2.1–11.
66. 1 Timothy 2.15.
67. Ephesians 5.22–25.
68. 2 Samuel 13.1.
69. Genesis 29.17–18.
70. 1 Samuel 18.20; cf. Jeremiah 2.2.
71. 1 Kings 11.1–2.
72. Genesis 24.67.
73. 1 Samuel 1.5.
74. Ezekiel 24.16. See also Exodus 21.5; Deuteronomy 21.15; Judges 14.16; 16.15; 2 Chronicles 11.21; Proverbs 4.6.
75. Genesis 21.10–14.
76. Deuteronomy 24.1–4.
77. See also Jeremiah 3.1.
78. Later called a "get."

79. Deuteronomy 23.12–14; the New Revised Standard Version translates the phrase "anything indecent" here, but "something objectionable" in 24.1; similarly, the New Jewish Publication Society Translation has "anything unseemly" and "something obnoxious." The King James Version, on the other hand, renders them as "unclean thing" and "some uncleanness."

80. See Deuteronomy 22.22.

81. Matthew 1.19.

82. Exodus 21.8.

83. Leviticus 22.13; see also Numbers 30.9.

84. Deuteronomy 22.21.

85. Deuteronomy 22.19. The fine is double the bride-price for virgins (Deuteronomy 22.29), so there are not just compensatory but also punitive damages, as in other laws concerning property (Exodus 22.4, 7, 9).

86. See especially Sirach 42.9–14.

87. Deuteronomy 22.13, 19. As noted above, there was no penalty for bridegrooms who were not virgins.

88. Deuteronomy 22.28–29; compare Exodus 22.16–17.

89. Leviticus 21.7, 14; Ezekiel 44.22 further prohibits any priest from marrying a widow.

90. Malachi 2.13–14, 16; v. 15 is opaque and I have not translated it. See also Micah 2.9.

91. Jeremiah 3.8; see also Isaiah 50.1.

92. Ezra 10.2–3. The word translated "expel" can also have the nuance of "divorce"; compare Deuteronomy 24.2.

93. 1 Esdras 9.36.

94. Scholars call this source Q (from the German word *Quelle*, "source"). It is a hypothetical source—that is, it does not actually exist, but is the best explanation for why Matthew and Luke agree verbatim in many cases when

there is no corresponding parallel in Mark. Most
scholars think that Q consisted almost entirely of
sayings of Jesus, which had been collected and
translated into Greek before their use by Matthew
and Luke.

95. Mark 10.11–12.
96. Matthew 19.9.
97. Luke 16.18.
98. Mark 10.2–9.
99. See Exodus 8.15, 32; 9.34.
100. Matthew 5.31–32; the quotation is from Deuteronomy
24.1.
101. 1 Corinthians 7.10–11.
102. 1 Corinthians 7.12–15.
103. Par. 1650 (1997 edition).
104. Matthew 19.8, an expansion by Matthew to the passage
in Mark about the debate between Jesus and the
Pharisees quoted above.

**Chapter 4   Thou Shalt Not: Forbidden Sexual Relationships
in the Bible**

1. Ecclesiastes 9.9.
2. Exodus 19.1–2.
3. Exodus 20.14; Deuteronomy 5.18. Because different
religious traditions number the Ten Commandments
differently, for some this is the sixth commandment.
4. See Sirach 23.22–23.
5. Exodus 20.17. Some religious groups follow the slightly
different version of this commandment in Deuteronomy
5.21 and count it as two commandments. But the wife is
still linked with other property, even if it slightly elevates
her value, and perhaps her status, of the wife.
6. Micah 2.1–2. See also Exodus 34.24.

7. This is further illustrated by one of Job's many protestations of innocence, when he asserts that neither was his heart enticed by a woman, nor did he lie in wait at his neighbor's door, so that when the neighbor left he could sleep with his wife (Job 31.9).

8. Par. 2350–91 (1997 edition).

9. Matthew 5.27–28.

10. As is the following saying concerning divorce.

11. Leviticus 20.10.

12. Deuteronomy 22.22. The punishment is more severe than in some other ancient Near Eastern legal collections, where it was left to the aggrieved husband to decide what the punishment for his wife would be; the same punishment would then be given to the man. In a late addition to the Gospel of John, only the woman who committed adultery is about to be executed; there is no mention of the man (John 7.53–8.11).

13. 2 Samuel 11.1.

14. 2 Samuel 11.5.

15. See 1 Samuel 21.5. That the Ammonite campaign was a "holy war" is clear from the presence of the ark of the covenant on the battlefield (2 Samuel 11.11).

16. 2 Samuel 11.15.

17. 2 Samuel 12.1–4.

18. 2 Samuel 12.7.

19. Exodus 20.5.

20. Note also the association of adultery and theft in Proverbs 6.29–35.

21. Leviticus 18.20; see also 20.10, quoted above.

22. Leviticus 18.6–16.

23. Leviticus 18.16.

24. Deuteronomy 27.20; see also 22.30. Paul seems to have the same situation in mind in 1 Corinthians 5.1.

25. Exodus 21.7.
26. Compare Exodus 22.16–17.
27. Deuteronomy 25.5–6.
28. Genesis 38.8.
29. Tobit 6.14–15.
30. Not the usual mode of execution, which was stoning. Death by fire was specified for a man who had sex with both a woman and her mother (as well as for them), and for a priest's daughter who became a prostitute (Leviticus 21.9), and is reported elsewhere (Judges 15.6).
31. The Hebrew word can be translated either prostitution or promiscuity. Here it must mean the latter: all that Judah knows is that Tamar is pregnant. See further pp. 150–51.
32. See 1 Chronicles 2.4–5, 9–15; Ruth 4.18–22. It is no coincidence that the obligation to marry the wife of a deceased next of kin is central to the plot of the book of Ruth (see 2.20; 4.1–12).
33. Leviticus 18.16; 20.21.
34. Genesis 38.26.
35. 2 Samuel 13.1–22; see further pp. 149–50.
36. Leviticus 18.9; similarly 20.17; Ezckiel 22.11.
37. Genesis 20.12.
38. See also Genesis 12.10–20; 26.6–11.
39. Genesis 19.30–38.
40. Genesis 9.20–27.
41. Genesis 35.22.
42. Genesis 49.3–4. The text is extremely difficult.
43. Leviticus 18.19.
44. Leviticus 15.16. For holy war, see Deuteronomy 23.9–14; 1 Samuel 21.5; 2 Samuel 11.11. The same prohibition is also found in Exodus 19.15, as part of the preparation for the theophany at Sinai.

45. Leviticus 15.18.
46. Leviticus 12.2–5; 15.19–24; similarly Leviticus 20.18. In societies like that of ancient Israel, where women married soon after menarche and for the rest of their reproductive years were usually either pregnant or breast-feeding, they would have menstruated only infrequently, so ritual impurity resulting from menstruation would also have been relatively infrequent.
47. Leviticus 18.22–23.
48. Leviticus 20.13, 15–16. Exodus 22.19 does not call for the death of the innocent animal; see also Deuteronomy 27.21.
49. Leviticus 19.19; Deuteronomy 22.5, 9–11.
50. Just as if we were to ask them about their religion. As Wilfred Cantwell Smith famously showed in *The Meaning and End of Religion: A New Approach to the Religious Traditions of Mankind* (New York: Macmillan, 1963), the notion of religion as a distinct system of beliefs and practices is a modern one. In antiquity, what we now call "religion" was part of culture more broadly and not really distinguished from it.
51. I use the terminology suggested by Bernadette J. Brooten, who observes that "'homoeroticism' has a less fixed meaning than 'homosexuality' and is therefore better suited to studying the texts of a culture very different from the contemporary cultures of industrialized nations" (*Love Between Women: Early Christian Responses to Female Homoeroticism* [Chicago: University of Chicago Press, 1996], 8).
52. See 1 Samuel 16.1–13, and compare 1 Samuel 10.1.
53. See 2 Samuel 21.19, and compare 1 Samuel 17.
54. 1 Samuel 18.1; 20.17.
55. 2 Samuel 1.23, 26.

56. 1 Samuel 18.1–4.
57. 1 Samuel 20.41; see earlier 1 Samuel 20.8, 14, 17.
58. For example, 1 Samuel 10.1; 2 Samuel 19.39; Proverbs 24.26; 27.6; and, in the New Testament, Judas kissing Jesus (Mark 14.44–45 and parallels).
59. By this point in the narrative, David has been married to Michal, Abigail, and Ahinoam.
60. See 1 Kings 5.1, 12; 9.13. Amos 1.9 also refers to the "covenant of brothers" between Israel and Tyre.
61. For example: Tom Horner, *Jonathan Loved David: Homosexuality in Biblical Times* (Philadelphia: Westminster, 1978); Daniel Helminiak, *What the Bible Really Says about Homosexuality* (San Francisco: Alamo Square, 1994); Christopher A. Hubble, *Lord Given Lovers: The Holy Union of David and Jonathan* (Lincoln, NE: iUniverse, 2003).
62. Genesis 13.10.
63. Genesis 13.13.
64. Genesis 18.20.
65. Genesis 18.22–33.
66. Genesis 19.4–5.
67. See above, pp. 7–9.
68. Genesis 19.8.
69. Wisdom of Solomon 19.14. This book is one of the Apocrypha, considered part of the Bible by Roman Catholics and Eastern Orthodox Christians but not by Jews and most Protestants.
70. Phyllis Trible, *Texts of Terror: Literary-Feminist Readings of Biblical Narratives* (Philadelphia: Fortress, 1984), chapter 3.
71. Judges 19.22–24.
72. Judges 19.25–26.
73. Judges 19.27–29.
74. Judges 20.6.

75. Luke 10.8–12.
76. Ezekiel 16.49–50.
77. For example, Exodus 3.9; 22.23; Isaiah 5.7; Job 34.28; Psalm 9.12.
78. Isaiah 1.10, 16–17; see also Jeremiah 23.14.
79. This is a view held by many contemporary biblical scholars. It also happens to be an interpretation given by David M. Carr in his annotations on Genesis in a Bible that I edited (*The New Oxford Annotated Bible*, 3d ed., 2001; 2007). Both gay activists and opponents of homosexuality seized on this, the former arguing that in fact the Bible does not condemn homosexuality, and the latter (including the website of Concerned Women for America) suggesting that we were promoting a gay agenda. Both are wrong, for different reasons.
80. Many other passages refer to Sodom, but almost always with reference to its desolate landscape as a prototype of divine punishment without specifying what it had done. Third Maccabees 2.5 speaks of the arrogance and evil deeds of Sodom, and 2 Peter 2.6 of their lawlessness and impiety, but this vague language need not imply sodomy.
81. Almost certainly not the apostle Jude, one of Jesus's brothers (Mark 6.3).
82. Jude 5–7. The letter mentions angels again in verse 9, when it refers to the struggle between the angel Michael and Satan over Moses's body.
83. In another ancient source, the first-century CE Jewish historian Josephus (*Antiquities* 1.200–1), the sin is also inhospitality, but in the Testament of Naphtali 3.4, it is departing from the "order of nature"; see further n. 85.
84. Genesis 6.1–4, retold in expanded form in 1 Enoch 6–10. See further below, pp. 176–77.
85. The same two episodes are juxtaposed in Testament of

Naphtali 3.4–5, where both Sodom and the "watchers" (the angels of Genesis 6) deviated from the order of nature. Perhaps here, as in Jude 7, the sin of the men of Sodom was wanting to have sex with angels rather than just with other men.

86. 1 Kings 14.24; 15.12; 22.46; 2 Kings 23.7.

87. For example, New American Bible, New Revised Standard Version, Revised English Bible, New Jewish Publication Society Translation.

88. See Stephanie Lynn Budin, *The Myth of Sacred Prostitution in Antiquity* (New York: Cambridge University Press, 2008), for a full discussion.

89. The word's root means "set apart"; that which is "holy" is set apart for the deity. Perhaps its rare use for prostitutes, whether male or female, reflects their marginal rather than their sacred status.

90. Genesis 38.21; compare v. 15.

91. Leviticus 18.22.

92. Leviticus 20.13.

93. Leviticus 18.24.

94. 1 Corinthians 6.9–11.

95. The Greek word *pornoi* in v. 9 is usually translated "fornicators," but it can also mean "male prostitutes" and "sodomites." If it means the latter, then there are three rather than two words for male homoeroticism in the passage.

96. New Revised Standard Version, New American Bible, and King James Version, respectively.

97. New American Bible, Revised English Bible, and New Revised Standard Version, respectively.

98. Throughout his letters, when Paul quotes the Jewish scriptures, he does so from their Greek version, which is known as the Septuagint.

99. 1 Timothy 1.9–11.
100. Romans 1.26–27.
101. 1 Corinthians 11.14.
102. John 7.53–8.11.
103. John 20.2; 21.7, 20.
104. John 13.23.

Chapter 5   Folly in Israel: Rape and Prostitution

1. Along with two other additions to Daniel, Susanna no longer exists in Hebrew but survived in Greek. It thus is not part of the Jewish or Protestant canons, but it is canonical for Catholics and Orthodox Christians, like the other Apocryphal books.
2. Deuteronomy 19.18–19.
3. Deuteronomy 22.28–29.
4. Exodus 22.16–17.
5. Deuteronomy 22.23–27.
6. Genesis 34.2.
7. Although according to Genesis 17.12 and Leviticus 12.3 males are to be circumcised on the eighth day after birth, this passage along with Exodus 4.24–26 (see above, pp. 12–13) may indicate that, as in other cultures, circumcision was originally a puberty ritual and hence associated with marriage: having reached sexual maturity, a boy was initiated into adulthood by circumcision and was able to marry.
8. Judges 20.6; see also 19.23–24; New Revised Standard Version "vile outrage." The phrase is also used of sexual offenses in Deuteronomy 22.21; Jeremiah 29.23; and 2 Samuel 13.12, discussed on pp. 149–50. It has the nuance of sacrilege; see Joshua 7.15, where it characterizes a violation of the rule of holy war, according to which all booty was to be dedicated to Yahweh.

9. Genesis 49.5–7.
10. Genesis 38; see above, pp. 110–12.
11. 2 Samuel 13.12.
12. *znh.* Also translated as "fornication," it is used only of women who engaged in extramarital sex, not men.
13. Hosea 1.2, as translated in the King James Version, New Revised Standard Version, New Jewish Publication Society Translation, and others. Note that the Revised English Bible gets it right: "an unchaste woman."
14. Proverbs 7.10.
15. Jeremiah 3.3; Ezekiel 23.40; Genesis 38.14.
16. Joshua 2.1; 1 Kings 3.17.
17. Genesis 38.14, 21.
18. 2 Maccabees 6.4. See also 1 Kings 22.38; Isaiah 23.15–16; Hosea 4.13–14; and perhaps Deuteronomy 23.17.
19. See pp. 132–34.
20. Apparently that applied only to Israelites. Isaiah 23.18, employing a frequent metaphorical use of prostitution, says that the city of Tyre, a once-forgotten prostitute, will resume her trade and her "gift" will be dedicated to Yahweh.
21. Leviticus 19.29.
22. Exodus 21.7.
23. There may also be a religious stigma concerning prostitution in the regulations concerning marriage by priests. According to Leviticus 21.7, 13–14, priests in general, and especially the high priest, are prohibited from marrying any woman who is not a virgin: off-limits, because the priests are "holy to their God," are widows, divorced women, women who have been raped, and prostitutes. Because of its ambiguity, the last word could also refer to promiscuity rather than specifically to prostitution. Between these two laws is

another (21.9), concerning the daughter of a priest who is guilty of promiscuity or prostitution; like Tamar in Genesis 38.24, she is to be burned to death. In any case, she has defiled her father, making him unable to perform his ritual functions. See also Amos 7.17.

24. 1 Corinthians 6.12–20.
25. Proverbs 29.3; see also 23.27–28; Sirach 9.6; 19.2; Luke 15.30.
26. Proverbs 6.26; see also Sirach 26.22.
27. Genesis 38; see further above, pp. 110–12.
28. Ruth 4.12, 18–22; Matthew 1.3.
29. Joshua 2.3.
30. In the Talmud, *b. Megillah* 14b.
31. Matthew 1.5; compare Ruth 4.21–22.
32. Judges 11.2. The situation resembles that of Hagar and Sarah, and of Abimelech's mother, who was Gideon's secondary wife or concubine (Judges 8.31).
33. Judges 14.14.
34. Judges 14.18.
35. Compare Genesis 29.22–30 and 1 Samuel 18.17–29.
36. Judges 16.23–30. The word translated "entertain" (v. 25) is the same Hebrew root meaning "to laugh" used in connection with Isaac, and has sexual innuendo; see pp. 75–77.
37. 1 Kings 3.16–28.
38. See Mark 2.15–16 and parallels; see also Luke 15.30.
39. Matthew 21.31–32.
40. Luke 7.37–38. In other accounts of a woman anointing Jesus (Matthew 26.6–7; Mark 14.3; in both cases his head rather than his feet), she is not called a sinner, and in John 12.3 she is identified as Mary of Bethany, the sister of Lazarus and Martha.

41. Nahum 3.4; Isaiah 23.16.
42. Revelation 17.5; see also 19.2.

Chapter 6   Fire in the Divine Loins: God's Wives in Myth and Metaphor

1. Ezekiel 1.1.
2. Ezekiel 10.20.
3. 2 Kings 2.11.
4. Ezekiel 1.27.
5. Ezekiel 1.28.
6. 1 Kings 12.10.
7. Bernhard W. Anderson, *Understanding the Old Testament* (Upper Saddle River, NJ: Prentice Hall, 5th ed., 2006), xviii.
8. Tikva Frymer-Kensky, *In the Wake of the Goddesses: Women, Culture, and the Biblical Transformation of Pagan Myth* (New York: Free Press, 1992), 189.
9. Here are some examples: *Eyes*: 2 Chronicles 16.9. *Ears*: 1 Samuel 8.21; 2 Samuel 22.7; 2 Kings 19.16; Nehemiah 1.6; Psalms 17.6; 34.15. *Heart*: Genesis 6.6; 8.21; 1 Samuel 13.14; Psalm 33.11. *Nose*: Especially in the idiom "his nose grew hot," meaning "became angry": Exodus 4.14; Numbers 25.4; Isaiah 5.25; etc. See also Genesis 8.21. *Arms*: Deuteronomy 4.34; Isaiah 51.9. *Feet*: Exodus 24.10; Isaiah 60.13; Ezekiel 43.7. *Backside*: Exodus 33.23.
10. Exodus 3.1 (here called Midian); Deuteronomy 33.1 (Sinai, Seir, Mount Paran); Judges 5.4 (Seir, Edom); Habakkuk 3.3 (Teman, Paran); Habakkuk 3.7 (Cushan, Midian).
11. See, for example, 1 Kings 18.19; 2 Kings 23.4–7.
12. In most drawings of this figure, she also has a phallus, leading to identification of her and the deity on her right as images of the Egyptian dwarf god Bes, who is sometimes depicted as hermaphroditic. While both

figures may have been influenced by depictions of Bes, there is in fact no phallus on the smaller figure, as careful examination of the photograph shows.

13. Isaiah 43.11; 44.6, 8; 45.5, 21. Scholars call Isaiah 40–55 "Second Isaiah."

14. Exodus 20.3.

15. Joshua 24.14; Ezekiel 20.5–8.

16. Judges 2.11–13.

17. Psalm 82.1.

18. Exodus 12.12.

19. 2 Kings 21.7; 23.6–7.

20. Jeremiah 44.15–19; see also 7.17–18.

21. Genesis 1.26–27.

22. Genesis 5.3.

23. Job 1.6; 2.1; 38.7; Psalms 29.1; 89.6; see also Deuteronomy 32.8.

24. Genesis 6.1–4. The "Nephilim" (literally, "fallen ones") are mentioned again in Numbers 13.32–33, where they are described as giants who inhabited the land of Canaan prior to the Israelites' arrival. (See also Deuteronomy 2.10–11; 3.11.)

25. Respectively: New Revised Standard Version; New English Bible; New Jewish Publication Society Translation; New American Bible.

26. Proverbs 8.22–31.

27. Wisdom of Solomon 8.3.

28. Philo, *De cherubim* 14.49.

29. Wisdom of Solomon 7.29.

30. Sirach 24.2; Proverbs 9.1.

31. Sirach 24.23; see also Baruch 4.1: "She is the book of God's commandments, the law that endures forever. All who possess her will live, but those who abandon her will die."

32. Luke 1.35.
33. See above, p. 69, and p. 210, n. 20.
34. Hosea 2.19–20. In Hosea these verses are words to be used in renewal of the relationship, but they were probably an ancient formula of engagement, which was a contractual relationship with more significance than in our culture. Legally, after the betrothal, cohabitation could take place, as the use here of the verb "to know" suggests.
35. Adapted from Isaiah 62.4–5, in which again a restoration of the relationship is the actual context.
36. Jeremiah 2.2.
37. Exodus 20.5; 34.14; Deuteronomy 4.24; 5.9; 6.15; Joshua 24.19; Nahum 1.2.
38. Hosea 2.3, 10.
39. Jeremiah 2.23–24, 30; 13.26.
40. In Ezekiel 16.21, Yahweh mentions "my children."
41. Ezekiel 16.37–42.
42. Ezekiel 16.62.
43. Jeremiah 3.12.
44. Hosea 2.14–15.
45. Revelation 21.2.
46. Ezekiel 23.48.
47. *Battered Love: Marriage, Sex, and Violence in the Hebrew Prophets* (Minneapolis, MN: Fortress, 1995), 86.

Conclusion

1. To be sure, different religious groups have canons that vary in both order and content. Jews, of course, do not include the New Testament in their Bibles, and within Christianity the Protestant canon is less inclusive than those of Roman Catholicism and the Eastern Orthodox churches. But the agreements are much more striking: all the books of the Hebrew Bible are part of every

Christian canon, and Christians agree completely on the
canonical books of the New Testament. Over the ages,
individuals, such as Marcion in the second century CE
and Thomas Jefferson in the nineteenth (not to mention
The Reader's Digest Bible [1982]), have tried to shorten the
canon by eliminating parts or even whole books they
considered no longer authoritative. Not surprisingly, all
these attempts have failed.

2. New York: Knopf, 2005.
3. Breyer, p. 15.
4. Breyer, p. 74.
5. Breyer, p. 98.
6. Breyer, p. 134.
7. Archibald Cox, *The Court and the Constitution* (Boston: Houghton Mifflin, 1987), 375–76.
8. Exodus 20.2; Deuteronomy 5.6.
9. Exodus 22.21; 23.9; Deuteronomy 5.15; 10.19; 15.15; etc.
10. Deuteronomy 5.14–15.
11. Babylonian Talmud, *Shabbat* 31a.
12. Matthew 7.12; compare Luke 6.31.
13. To be sure, just as constitutional scholars may disagree with Breyer's formulation, the criterion I have articulated is not the only possible one. But in both cases, I think, it is essential to establish one or more explicit criteria for applying an old text to new contexts, not just to appeal to original or literal meaning.
14. Leviticus 19.18.
15. Matthew 22.34–40; Mark 12.28–31.
16. Romans 13.9–10; see also Galatians 5.14; James 2.8.

INDEX

Aaron, 43, 72
Abel, 45
Abigail, 53–54
Abihail, 22
Abimelech, 77
Abiram, 30
Abishag, 81–82
Abner, 81
abortion, 64–67
Abraham (Abram), xiv, 74–77
  Keturah and, 78
  Rebekah and Isaac, 27–28,
    67–68, 76–77
  sacrifice of Isaac, 31–32
  Sarah and, 24, 74–76, 77, 84,
    112–13
  Sodom and, 122–23
Absalom, 8, 45, 81, 115, 150
abstinence, as an ideal, 32–36
Achilles, 120
acrostics, 50–52
*Active Liberty: Interpreting Our
    Democratic Constitution*
    (Breyer), 191–92
Adah, 78
Adam and Eve, 57, 212n
  sexual connotation of "knowing"
    and, 7–9
Adam and Eve (Klimt), 2
Adonijah, 82, 115
adultery, 86, 101–8, 216n
  David and Bathsheba, 104–8
Ahab, 71–72
Ahaz, 30
Ahaziah, 47–48

Ai, 22
Akiva ben Joseph, 17
Ammonites, 29–30, 113
Amnon, 83, 112–13, 149–50
Amos, 7–8
Amoz, 22
Anna, 46
annulments, 97–98
"apostles," 49, 58
arranged marriages, 67–70, 82–84
Asa of Judah, 47
Asenath, 211n
Asherah, 47, 71–72, 167–70,
    172–75
Athaliah, 47–48
Atum, 166
Auden, W. H., 15

Baal, 47, 71–72, 165–66
Barak, 46
Baruch, xiii, 226n
Barzillai, 8–9
Bathsheba, 22, 81–82, 104–8, 145
Benjamin, 128
Ben Sira, 28, 55, 212n
berît, 69
Bes, 225–26n
bestiality, 116
Bethuel, 68
Bible
  formation of, xii–xv
  inconsistencies in, xiv–xvi, 38–39,
    72, 89
  sources, xiii–xiv
  use of term, xii–xiii

biblical scholarship, and bias, 54–58
Bilhah, 78, 114
Bill of Rights, 190
birth control, 64–65
Boaz, 11, 72, 155
bodies, descriptions of, in Song of Solomon, 4–6, 16–18
Book of the Wars of the Lord, xiii
Breyer, Stephen, 191–92
bride-price, 25–26, 28, 68–69, 147
Brooten, Bernadette J., 218n

Cain, 7, 78
Cana, wedding at, 83
Canaan (Canaanites), 11–12, 113, 133, 135, 165–66
Carr, David M., 220n
Carter, Jimmy, 59–60
Catechism of the Catholic Church, 97, 103–4
"category confusion," 116–17, 132, 138
celibacy, as an ideal, 32–36
cherubim, 163
children of Yahweh, 176–78
child sacrifice, 31–32
circumcision, 13, 222n
Cogan, Mordechai, 213n
community and foundational texts, 192–93
"concubines," 80
Constitution, U.S., 190–92, 195
Coogan, Matthew, 204n
Corinthians, xiii, 95, 98, 136–37
"covenant," 181–82
"covet," 103
Cox, Archibald, 192
Creed of the Council of Nicaea, 38–39
cylinder seal, 162

Daniel, 143–45
David, 80–83
  Abigail and Nabal, 53–54
  Barzillai and, 8–9
  Bathsheba and, 104–8
  Jonathan and, 118–21
  killing of the Philistines, 40
  Michal and Saul, 68, 83
  royal harem of, 8–9, 80–83, 115
  Solomon and, 81–82
  Tamar and, 112, 149–50
  "wise" women and, 44–45
"deacons," 49
Dead Sea Scrolls, 14–15, 33
death by fire, 217n
death penalty. See also stoning
  for adultery, 104
Deborah, 40, 43–44, 46
Decalogue (Ten Commandments), xiv, 101–4, 182, 193, 215n
Delilah, 157
descent and inheritance, 22–23
Deuteronomy, 87, 92–94, 96, 97, 110, 111, 112, 132, 134, 135, 146–47, 151, 215n
diakonos, 49
dietary laws, 116, 152
"dildo," 15
Dinah, 68, 147–49
disinheritance, 29
divorce, 29, 84–98
  in book of Malachi, 88–90, 97
  Jesus and, 91–98
  laws addressing, 85–88, 145–46
"dog," 134
domestic roles of women, 50–60
  biblical scholarship and, 54–58
  ideal wife, 50–52
Donne, John, 10

eating, as euphemism for sex, 9
Ecclesiastes, 101, 152
ejaculation, 110, 115–16
El, 165
Elhanan, 118–19
Eliam, 22
Elijah, 26–27, 47
Elizabeth, 36–37, 74, 210n

INDEX

Elkanah, 78, 84
elohim, 175–76
endogamy, 70–73, 90, 148
Endor, 41–43
Enkidu, 120
Enlil, 166
Enosh, 23
Er, 110
erotic love poem, in Song of
    Solomon, 4–6, 16–18
Esau, 69, 71, 78
Essenes, 33
Esther, 22, 55–56, 72–73, 145
etiology, 114–15, 122
eunuchs, 35
Euodia, 49
euphemisms, 15–16
    for sexual acts and organs, 7–16
Evangelical Lutheran Church,
    and same-sex relationships,
    xi–xii
Exodus, 43–44, 87, 101–2, 135,
    193–94
exogamy, 70–73, 89–90
"eye for eye, tooth for tooth," 65
Ezekiel, xiv, 16, 84, 129–30, 163–65,
    183–86, 187, 212*n*
Ezra, 89

family members, sex with, 108–15
    Lot's daughters, 113
    Reuben, 114–15
    Tamar, 110–13
"family values," xvi, 188
"feet," 11–14
feminist biblical scholarship, 54–55,
    57–58
"flesh," 14
"folly in Israel," 87, 128, 147, 148
forbidden sexual relationships,
    101–40. *See also* same-sex
    relationships
    adultery, 101–8
    sex with family members, 108–15
"fornication," 223*n*

Gabriel, 37
Gad, 114
Garden of Eden, 21–22, 78
    sexual connotation of "knowing,"
    7–9
gender issues, 21. *See also* status of
    women
genealogical connections, 22–23
Genesis, 21–23, 78, 93–94, 110,
    112–13, 175
genitals, euphemisms for, 11–15
Gentileschi, Artemisia, *142*
Gibeah, 125–28
Gideon, 78
Gilead, 29, 155
Gilgamesh, 120
Go-Between, The (Hartley), 3
Goddess Wisdom, 178–81
gold amulet from ancient Ugarit,
    174
Golden Calf, 211–12*n*
Goliath, 118–19
Gomer, 150–51
Gomorrah, 121–22, 124, 131–32
"great whore Babylon," 159

Hagar, 70–71, 74–75, 77, 84, 86
Ham, 113
Hamor, 68
"hand," 14–15
Hannah, 74, 84
Hartley, L. P., 3
Heber the Kenite, 11–12, 22
Helen of Troy, 180
Helminiak, Daniel, 219*n*
Herodotus, 133
Hezekiah, 82
Hiel, 30
Hillel the Elder, 194
Hiram, 121
Holofernes, 46
homoeroticism, 117–18, 218*n*.
    See also same-sex relationships
"homosexuality," 117. *See also*
    same-sex relationships

231

"Honor your father and your
    mother," 52–53
Horner, Tom, 219n
Hosea, 69, 150–51, 182–83, 185,
    227n
hospitality
    Gibeah and, 125–28
    Jesus and, 128–29
    Sodom and, 124–25, 129–30
Hours of Marguerite de Coetivy,
    100
Hubble, Christopher A., 219n
Huldah, 44
human sacrifice, 30–32
    Jephthah's virgin daughter,
        28–30, 32, 39–40

ideal wife, 50–52
Iliad, 120
incest, 108–15
    Lot's daughters, 113
    Reuben, 114–15
    Tamar, 110–13
infant mortality, 24, 64–65, 67
inheritance and descent, 22–23, 29
inhospitality. See hospitality
intergenerational guilt, 108
Isaac, 71, 75–77
    Abraham's sacrifice of, 31–32
    Rebekah and, 27–28, 67–68,
        76–77, 84
    root meaning of name, 75–76
Isaiah, 11, 15, 22, 44, 130
Ishmael, 70–71, 75, 77, 84
Israel, as Yahweh's wife, 181–88

Jackson, Shirley, 144
Jacob
    Bilhah and, 77–78, 114
    bride-price and, 68–69
    Dinah and Shechem, 147–49
    Leah and, 10, 69, 71, 78, 114
    Rachel and, 10, 69, 71, 77–78, 83,
        114
Jael, 11–12, 22, 46

James, 39
Jefferson, Thomas, 228n
Jehoiachin, 212n
Jehoram, 47
Jephthah, 28–30, 32, 39–40, 155
Jeremiah, xiii, 82, 89, 172–73, 182,
    185, 209–10n
Jericho, 10, 31, 154
Jerusalem, 8, 105–6, 159, 183–86
Jesus
    adultery and, 104
    celibacy and, 34–35
    as divine father's only child, 176
    divorce and, 91–98
    God's sacrifice of, 32
    hospitality and, 128–29
    Mary's conception of, 36–39
    presence of women among
        followers of, 55, 56, 57–58
    prostitutes and, 158–59
    same-sex relationships and, 139–40
    Sermon on the Mount, 95, 104
    siblings of, 39, 206–7n
Jezebel, 47, 71–72
Joab, 44–45, 105, 107
Joakim, 143
Job, 66–67, 152, 216n
John, 35–36, 139
John the Baptist, 36–37, 74, 159,
    210n
Jonathan, 118–21
Jonson, Ben, 15
Joseph, 37–38, 39, 72, 86, 211n
Josephus, 220n
Joshua, 16, 22, 31, 154–55
Josiah, 44
Judah (kingdom), 82, 89
Judah (patriarch), 72, 110–12,
    133–34, 153
Jude, 130–32
Judean fertility figurines, 170
Judges, 11–12, 28–29, 129–30, 155,
    171
Judith, 46, 145
Junia, 48–49

INDEX

Keturah, 78
kiss (kissing), 120
Klimt, Gustav, *2*
"know" ("knowing"), 7–9
Kuntillet Ajrud, 166–70

Laban, 68, 69, 210*n*
Lamech, 78
"laughter," 75–77, 179
"law of talion," 65
leadership and women, 46–49, 56
Leah, 10, 69, 71, 78, 114, 147
Leda, 180
lesbian relationships, 135, 138
Levi, 147–49
Levite, 125–28, 187
Leviticus, 108–12, 115–16, 134–35, 139
"liberty and justice for all," 195
"life for life" principle, 65
Lilith, 212*n*
loins, 164–65
Lot, 113, 122–25, 129
"Lottery, The" (Jackson), 144
"love," 83, 120–21
love, and marriage, 63–64
Luke, 36–37, 38, 46, 90–93

Maacah, 47
Mahalath, 71
Maher-shalal-hash-baz, 44, 207*n*
Malachi, 88–90, 97
male bonding, 120
"man," 204*n*
Manasseh, 30
mandrakes, 10
Manoah, 74
Marcion of Sinope, 228*n*
Mark, 90–93, 94
marriage, 63–84
    abortion, 64–67
    arranged, 67–70, 82–84
    endogamy and exogamy, 70–73
    polygamy, 73–84
    status of women in, 25–26

marriage contracts, 69–70, 102, 210*n*
Mary (mother of Jesus), 36–39, 86, 181
Mary Magdalene, 139, 159, 208*n*
Mary of Bethany, 224*n*
Massachusetts Constitution, xii
"master," 24
masturbation, 110
Matthew, 35, 37–38, 39, 90–93, 94–95, 97, 104, 159
Meaning and End of Religion, The (Smith), 218*n*
menstruation (menstrual cycle), 14, 115–16, 218*n*
Mesha, 30
metaphor, 165–66
    Yahweh's wives in, 181–88
mezuzah, 13
Micah, 103
Michal, 68, 83
Milton, John, 177–78
Miriam, 43, 72
Mirror of Human Salvation, 20
miscarriages, 65, 67
mistresses, 80
mixed marriages, 71–73
mixing categories, 116–17, 132, 138
Moabites, 113
monogamy, xii
monotheism, 171–72, 176, 180
Mormons, and polygyny, 79
Moses, xiv, 12–13, 43, 68, 72, 93, 167, 193, 207*n*
Mount Sinai, 167
murder (homicide), 137, 147, 195
myth, 165–66
    Yahweh's wives in, 166–70

Nabal, 53–54
Naboth, 47
Nahor, 27
"nakedness," 10–11, 108–9

INDEX

"nakedness of a thing," 86, 92, 95
Naomi, 27
Naphtali, 114
Nathan, 107
"navel," 203n
necromancy, 41–43
Nehemiah, 44, 89
neighbor, love of, 127, 195
neonatal mortality, 24, 67
"Nephilim," 226n
Nineveh, 159
Ninlil, 166
Noadiah, 44
Noah, 113
Numbers, xiii
Nun, 22
Nympha, 48

Onan, 110
"onanism," 110
Origen, 35
orphans, 26, 129

Paradise Lost (Milton), 178
patriarchal bias, 22–25, 187
    marriage and, 63–64, 70
    status of women and, 54–60
Patroclus, 120
Paul, xiii, 195
    birth of Jesus and, 38
    celibacy and, 33–35
    divorce and, 95–97
    homoerotic relationships and,
        135–38
    prostitution and, 152
    status of women and, 55–59
    women leaders and, 48–49
Pauline privilege, 98
Perez, 111
Petrine privilege, 98
phallus (penis), 14–15, 225–26n
pharmakeia, 209n
Philip, 46
Philistines, 40, 41–42, 119, 155–57
Philo, 179

Phoebe, 49
placenta, 11
polygamy (polygyny), 63, 73–84
    Abraham and, 74–77
    Jacob and, 77–78
    laws addressing, 79–80
    Mormons and, 79
    in the New Testament, 82–83
    royal harems, 8–9, 80–83
polytheism in ancient Israel,
    170–77
Pope, Marvin, 203n
"popular religion," 174–75
pornoi, 221n
postfeminist biblical scholarship,
    55–58
"primary" wives, 80
property, wives as, 24–26, 102, 215n
prophecy (prophets), 43–46
prostitution (prostitutes), 133–34,
    150–60, 223–24n
    in book of Proverbs, 152–53
    in book of Revelation, 159
    Gomer, 150–51
    Jephthah's mother, 155
    Jesus and, 158–59
    Paul and, 152
    Rahab, 10, 16, 154–55
    ritual purity and, 151–52
    Samson and, 155–57
    Solomon and, 157–58
    Tamar, 133–34, 153
Proverbs, 9, 152–53, 178–79
public roles of women, 39–49
    necromancy, 41–43
    prophecy, 43–46
    rulers, 46–49
    "wise" women, 44–45
"pudenda," 109

Q source, 214–15n

Rabbah, 105
Rachel, 10, 69, 71, 78, 83, 114
Rahab, 10, 16, 154–55

rape, 143–50
  of Dinah, 147–49
  Gibeah and, 125–28
  laws addressing, 145–47
  marriage and, 33
  Sodom and, 124
  of Susanna, 143–45
  of Tamar, 83, 149–50
  use of term, 145
Rebekah, 27–28, 67–68, 76–77, 84
Rehoboam, 164
religious ceremonies, women as
  participants in, 40–41
Reuben, 10, 114–15
Revelation, 35, 159
ritual purity, and prostitution, 151–52
Rizpah, 22
Roman Catholicism
  celibacy and, 35–36
  divorce and, 97–98
romance and marriage, 63–64
royal harems, 8–9, 80–83
rulers, women as, 46–49
Ruth, 11, 27, 55–56, 72

sacred prostitution, 133–34
Salome, 208n
Samaria, 47, 66, 167, 183, 184
same-sex relationships, xi–xii,
  117–40
  David and Jonathan, 118–21
  Jesus and, 139–40
  prohibitions of, 134–39, 220n
  Sodom, 121–34
Samson, 37, 74, 155–57
Samuel, 42–43, 78, 105, 118
Sarah (Sarai), 24, 74–77, 84, 86,
  111, 112–13
Sarah Bringing Hagar to Abraham
  (Stomer), 62
Saul, 41–43, 68, 81, 118–20
"secondary" wives, 80
Segub, 30
Sennacherib, 82
Sermon on the Mount, 95, 104

Seth, 23
sexual acts and organs,
  euphemisms for, 7–16
sexual orientation, 138
Shakespeare, William, 15
Sheba, 45
Shechem, 68, 147–50
Shelah, 111, 153
Shu, 166
Simeon, 46, 147–49
Sisera, 11–12, 46
slavery, 193–94
  women and, 25–26
Smith, Wilfred Cantwell, 218n
Sodom, 121–34, 220–21n
"sodomite," 132–34
sodomy, 130–34
Solomon, 80–83, 121, 124, 157–58
Song of Deborah, 12
Song of Moses, 207n
Song of Solomon, 4–6, 16–18, 58,
  63, 80, 145
Southern Baptist Convention,
  59–60
status of women, 21–60
  domestic roles, 50–60
  public roles, 39–49
  subordination, 22–25
  virginity, 27–39
  widows, 26–27
Stomer, Matthias, 62
stoning, 87, 144–45, 217n
subordination of women, 22–25.
  See also status of women
surrogate mothering, 77–78
Susanna, 143–45, 222n
Susanna and the Elders
  (Gentileschi), 142
Synoptic Gospels, 90–93
Syntyche, 49

Tamar
  incest and, 110–13
  prostitution and, 133–34, 153
  rape of, 83, 149–50

Tefnut, 166

Tekoa, 44–45

Teman, 167

Ten Commandments (Decalogue), xiv, 101–4, 182, 193, 215n

Terah, 23

Thomas, Dylan, 9

"Thou shalt not commit adultery," 102

Timothy, 137

Tobias, 70

Tobit, 70, 111

"to lie with" ("to sleep with"), 9–10

translation issues, 15, 16

tree of knowledge, 8, 9, 21–22

tree of life, 21–22

Tyre, 71, 159, 223n

Ugarit, 14, 174

"uncovering the nakedness," 10–11, 108–9, 112, 115

Uriah, 22, 106–7

U.S. Constitution, 190–92, 195

virginity, 27–39
    as an ideal, 32–36
    divorce and, 86–87
    Jephthah's virgin daughter, 28–30, 32, 39–40
    Mary, 36–39
    rape and, 146–47

Virgin Mary, 36–39, 86, 181

"vulva," 203n

Weems, Renita, 187

widows, 26–27

Wisdom (goddess), 178–81

"wisdom literature," 152–53

Wisdom of Solomon, 219n

"wise" women, 44–45

"witch," 41–42

wives of Yahweh
    in metaphor, 181–88
    in myth, 166–70

women, status of, 21–60
    domestic roles, 50–60
    public roles, 39–49
    subordination, 22–25
    virginity, 27–39
    widows, 26–27

"Yahweh and his Asherah," 167–70

Yeats, William Butler, 180

"You shall have no other gods apart from me," 171–72, 181

Zechariah, 36–37, 74

Zedekiah, 212n

Zeus, 180

Zillah, 78

Zilpah, 78, 114

Zipporah, 12–13, 211n

ABOUT THE AUTHOR

Michael Coogan is Professor of Religious Studies at Stonehill College, Lecturer on Old Testament/Hebrew Bible at Harvard Divinity School, and Director of Publications for the Harvard Semitic Museum. He is editor of *The New Oxford Annotated Bible,* and has edited and written several books on the Bible and its interpretation, including *The Old Testament: A Very Short Introduction.* He and his wife, Pamela Hill, live in Concord, Massachusetts.

ABOUT TWELVE
Mission Statement

TWELVE was established in August 2005 with the objective of publishing no more than one book per month. We strive to publish the singular book, by authors who have a unique perspective and compelling authority. Works that explain our culture; that illuminate, inspire, provoke, and entertain. We seek to establish communities of conversation surrounding our books. Talented authors deserve attention not only from publishers, but from readers as well. To sell the book is only the beginning of our mission. To build avid audiences of readers who are enriched by these works—that is our ultimate purpose.

For more information about forthcoming TWELVE books, please go to www.TwelveBooks.com.